DEER SONGS:
A CHICANO CODEX COLORING BOOK

BY ISRAEL F. HAROS LOPEZ

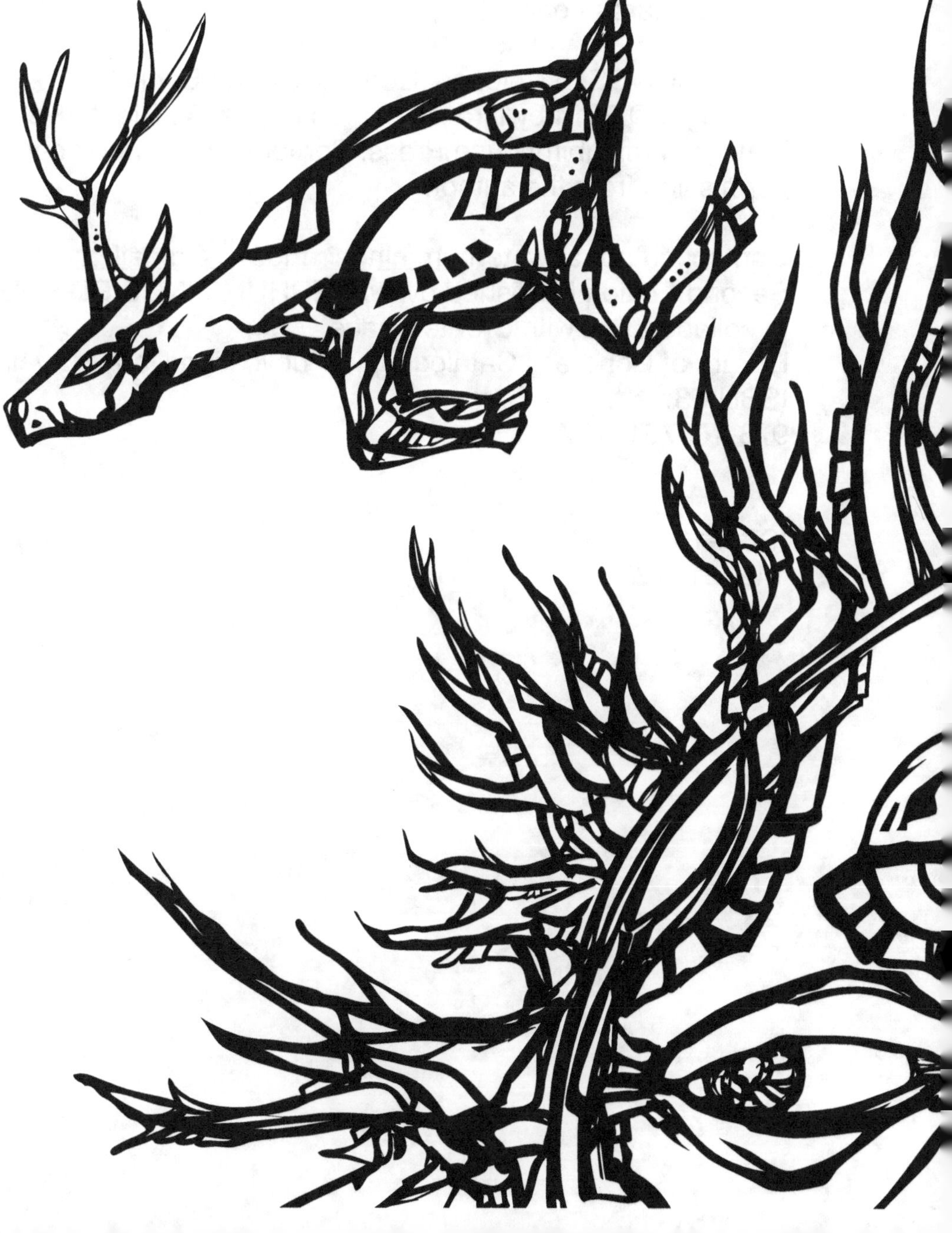

DEER SONGS: A Chicano Codex Coloring Book
Drawn by Israel F. Haros Lopez
Cover Design by
Israel F. Haros Lopez

Contact author at waterhummingbirdhouse@gmail.com
Second Edition Published by WATERHUMMINGBIRDHOUSE PRESS 2014
In collaboration with Create Space
Library of Congress Cataloging-in-Publication Data is available upon request
ISBN-13:
978-1497517127

ISBN-10:
1497517125

Para Maaso y Mario y Todos los Que Le Cantan y Bailan Con el Venado

A un lado de su rio
toma su agua sagrada
a su lado viento
a su lado tierra

Mazatl! Mazatl!
Mazatl! Mazatl!

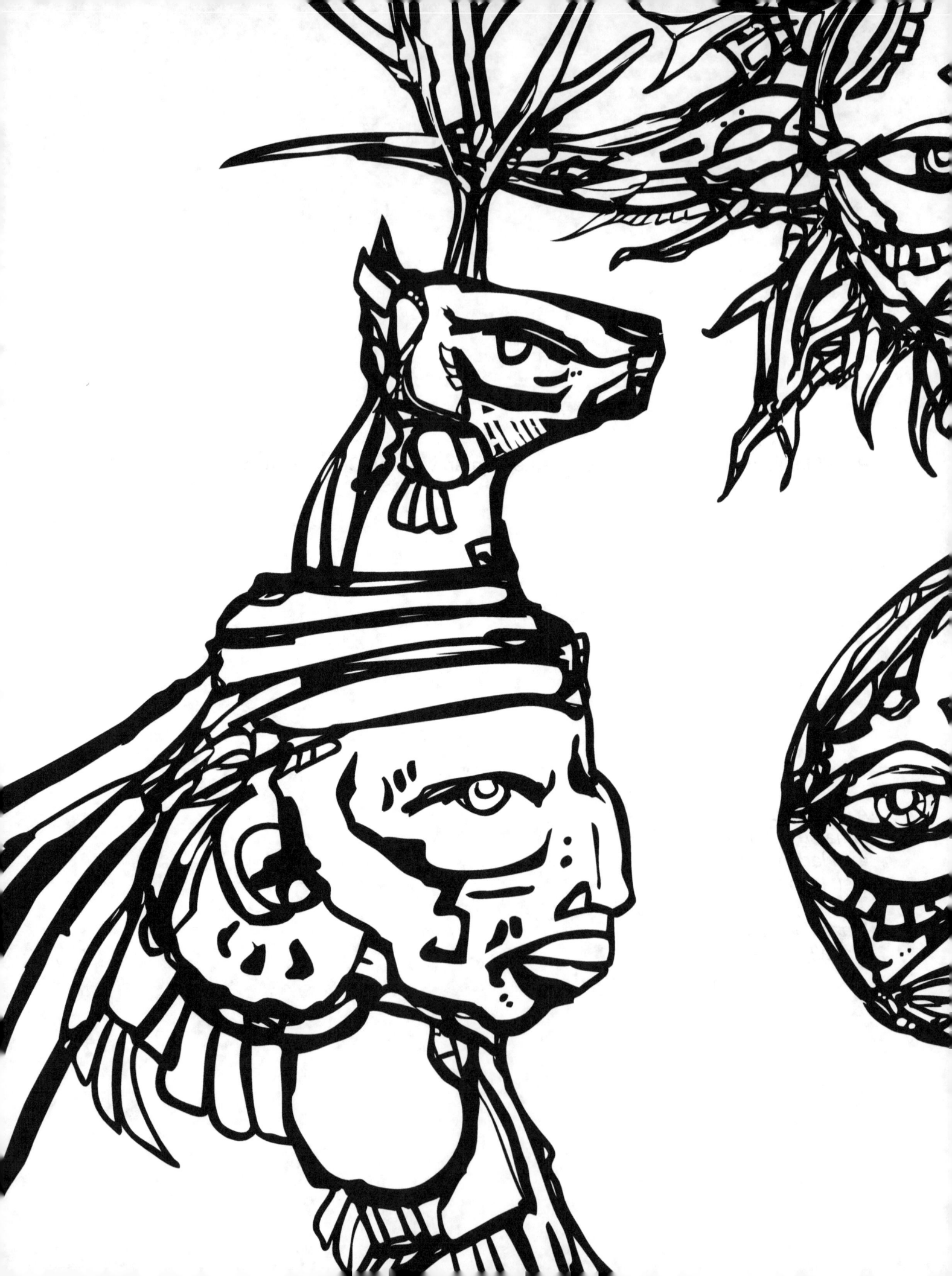

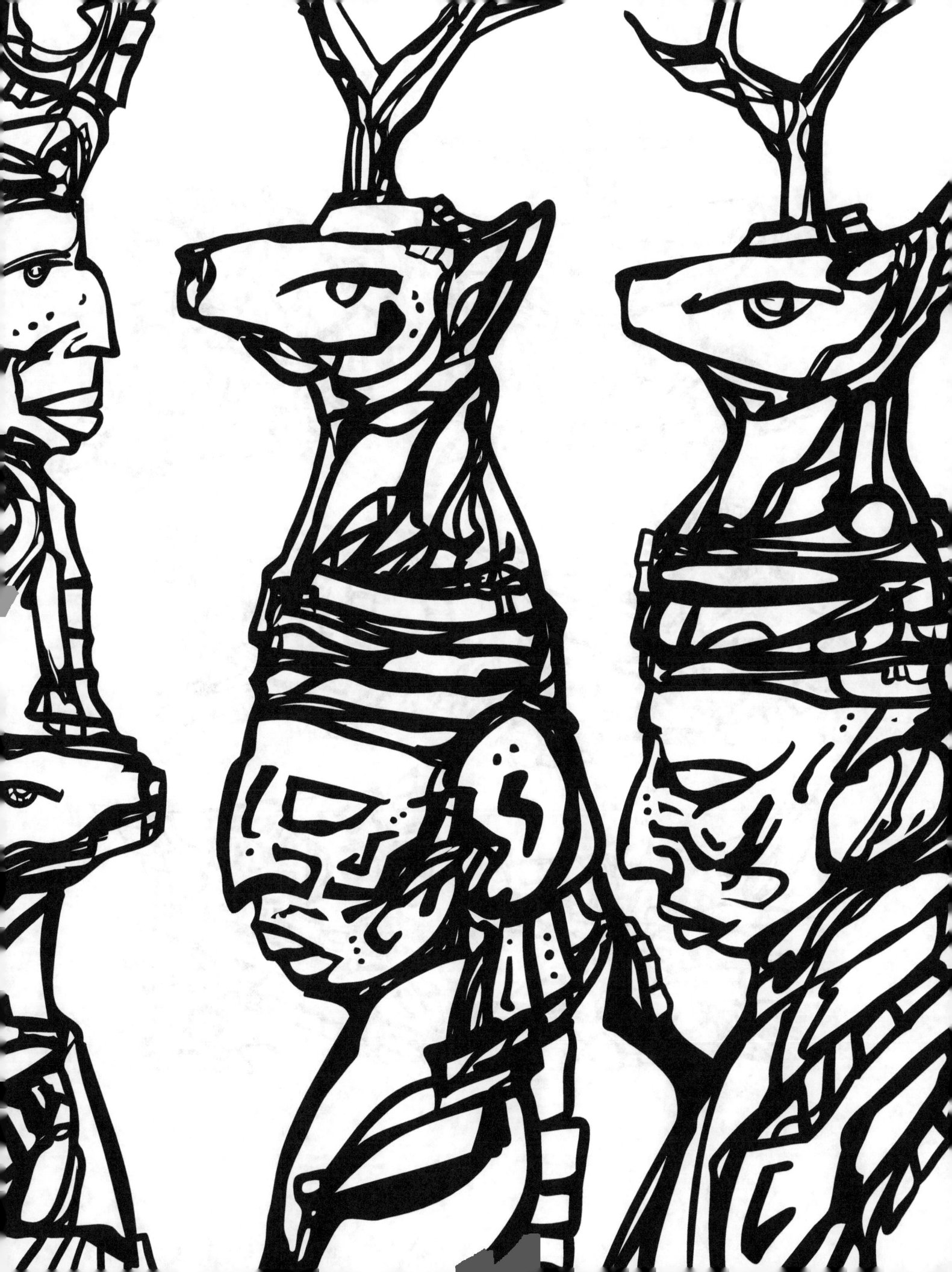

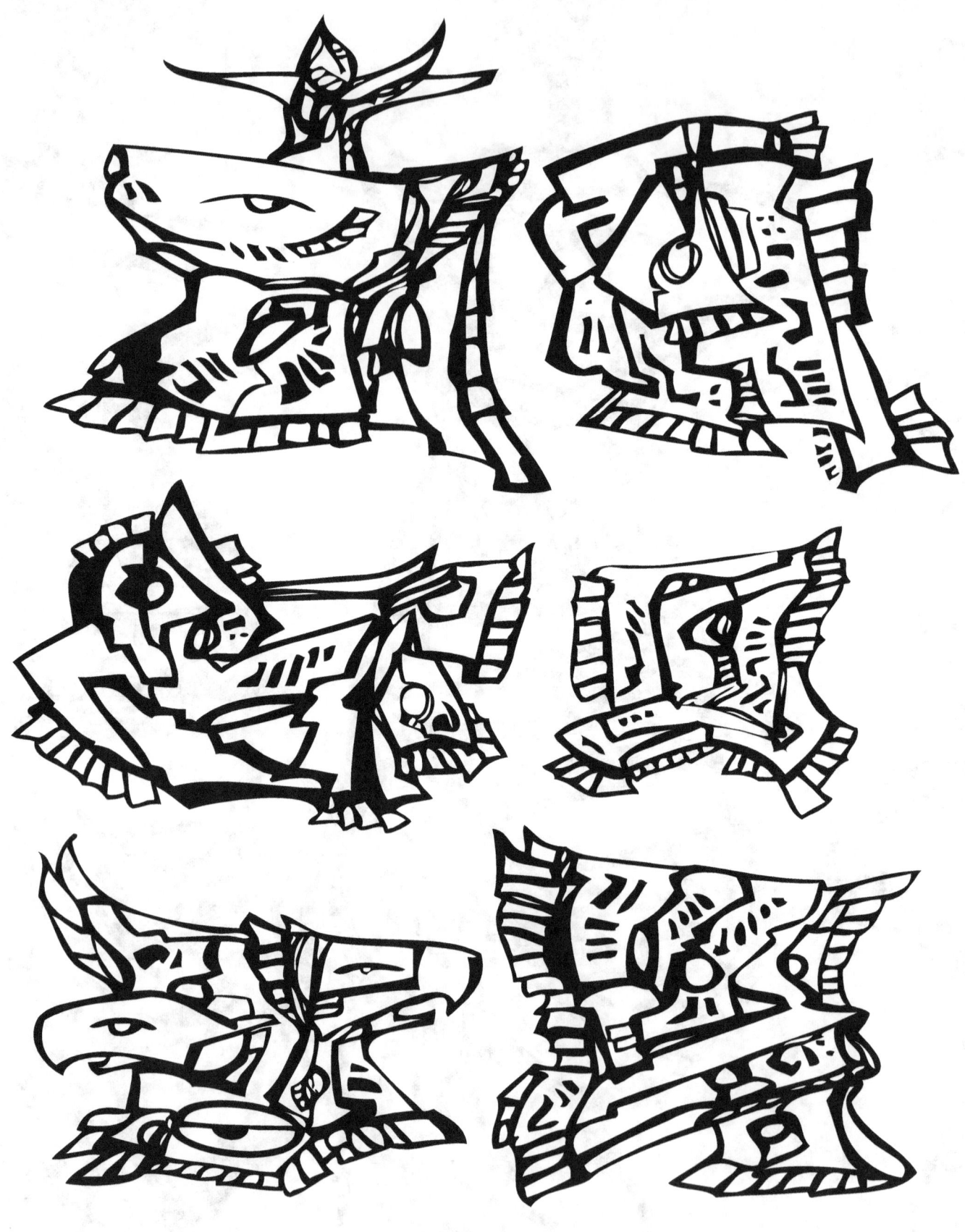

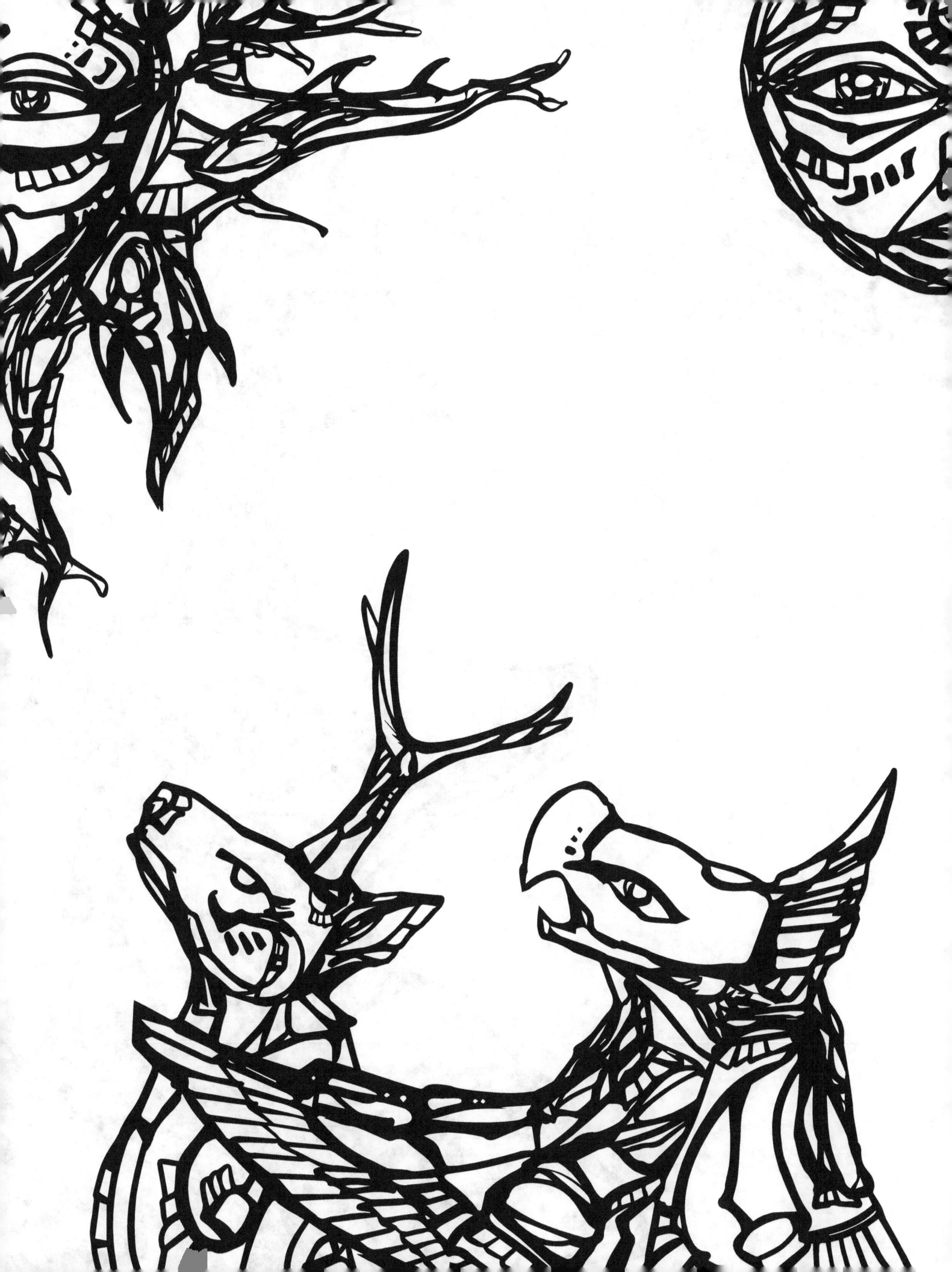

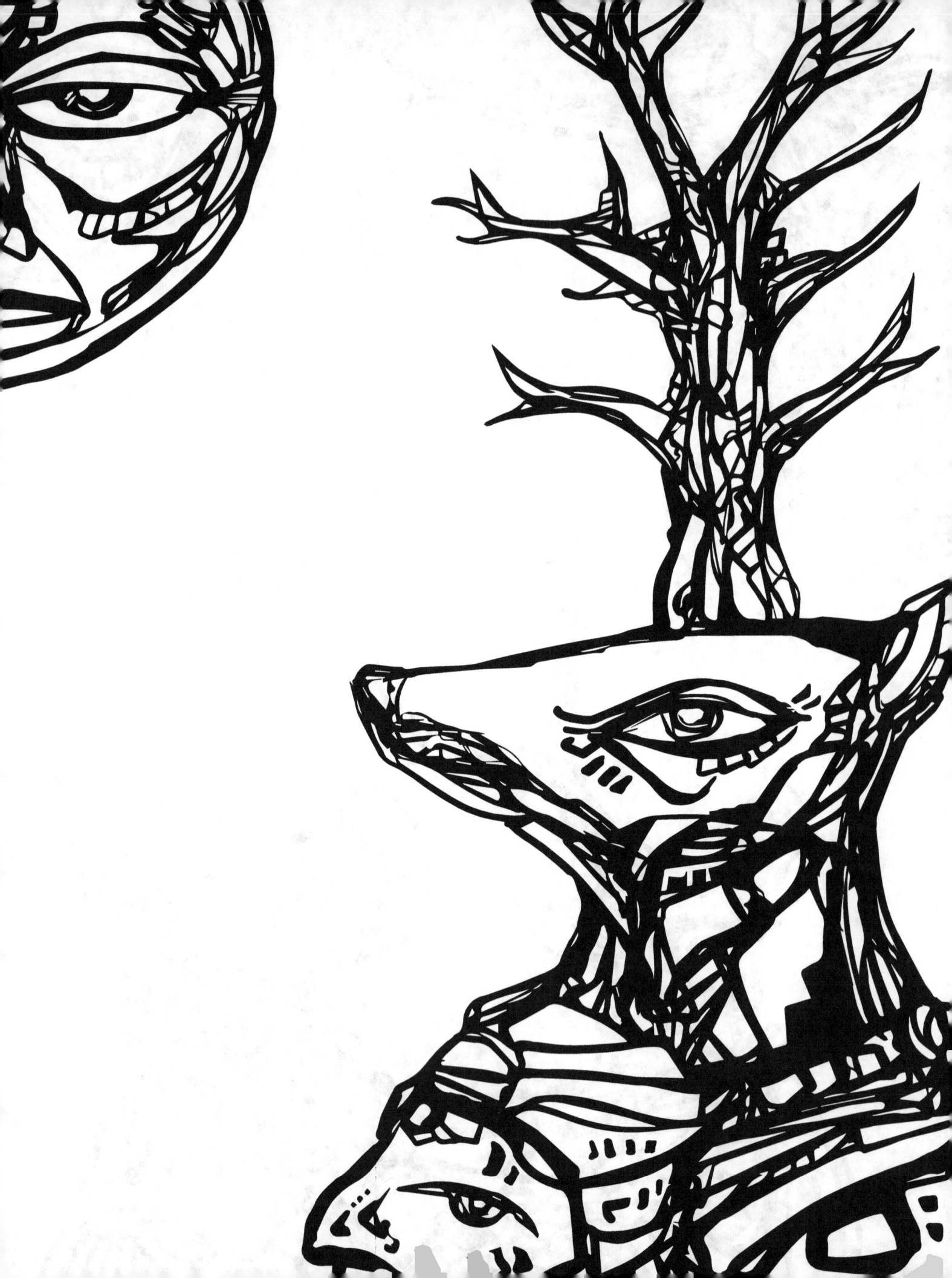

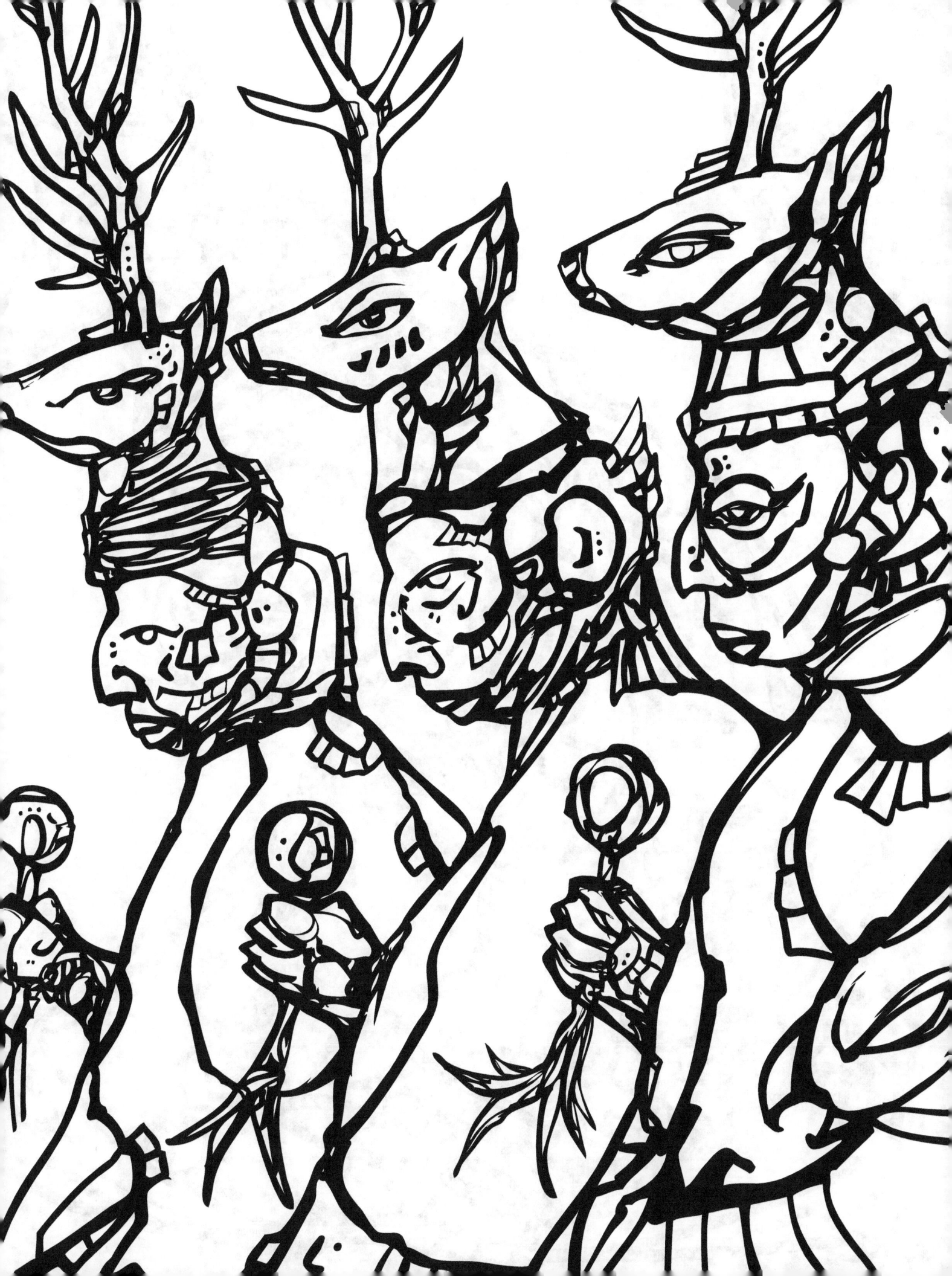

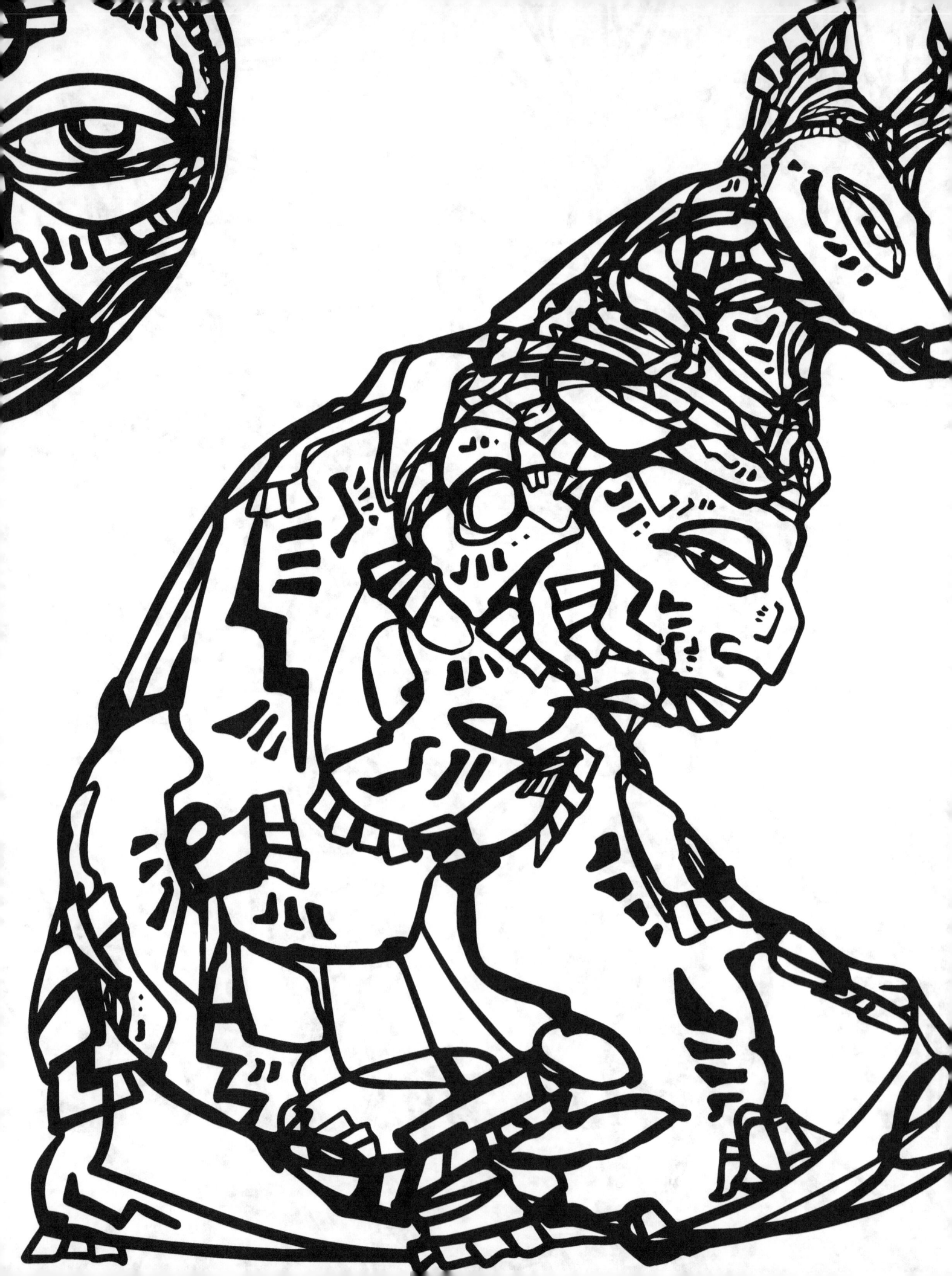

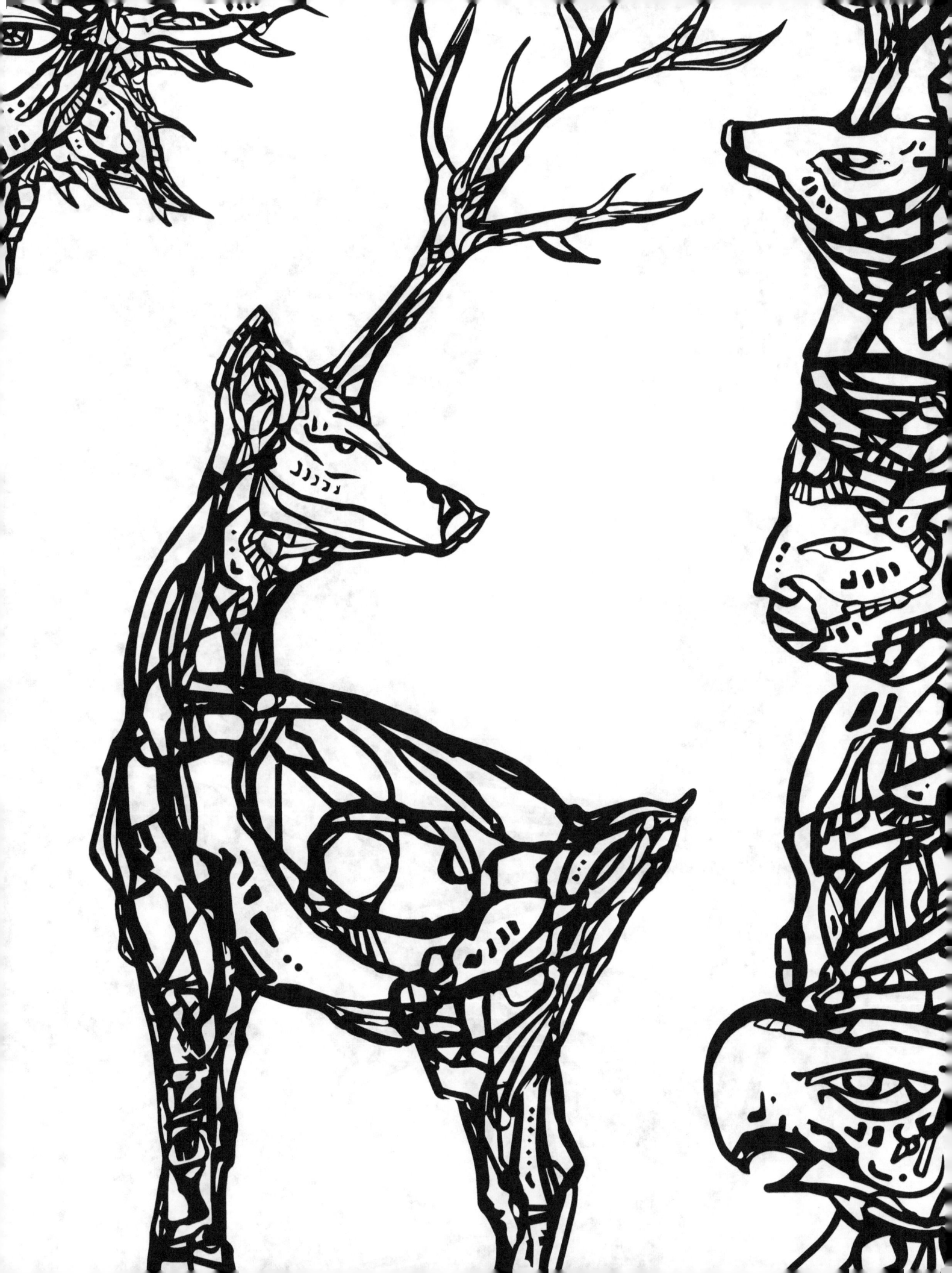

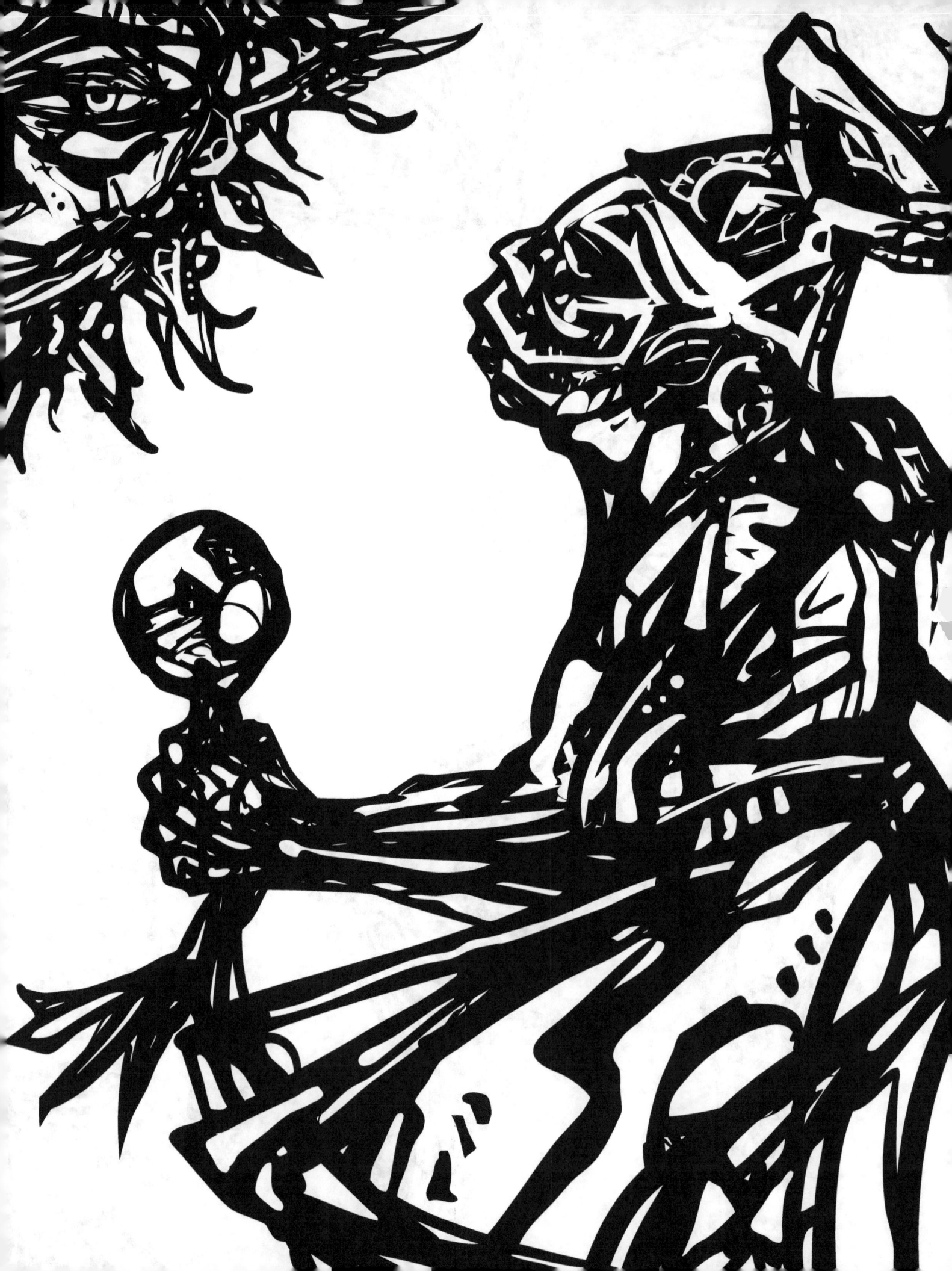

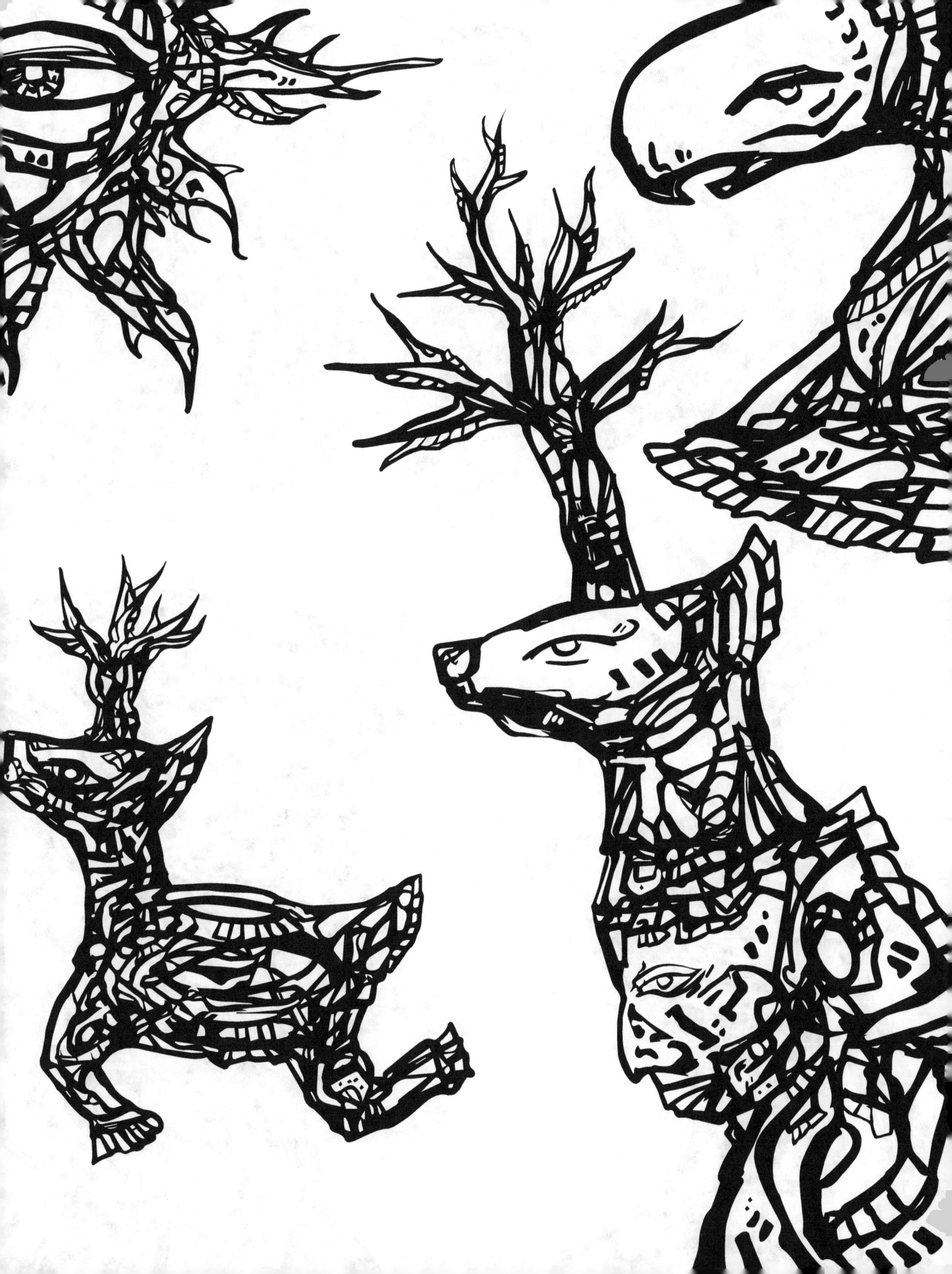

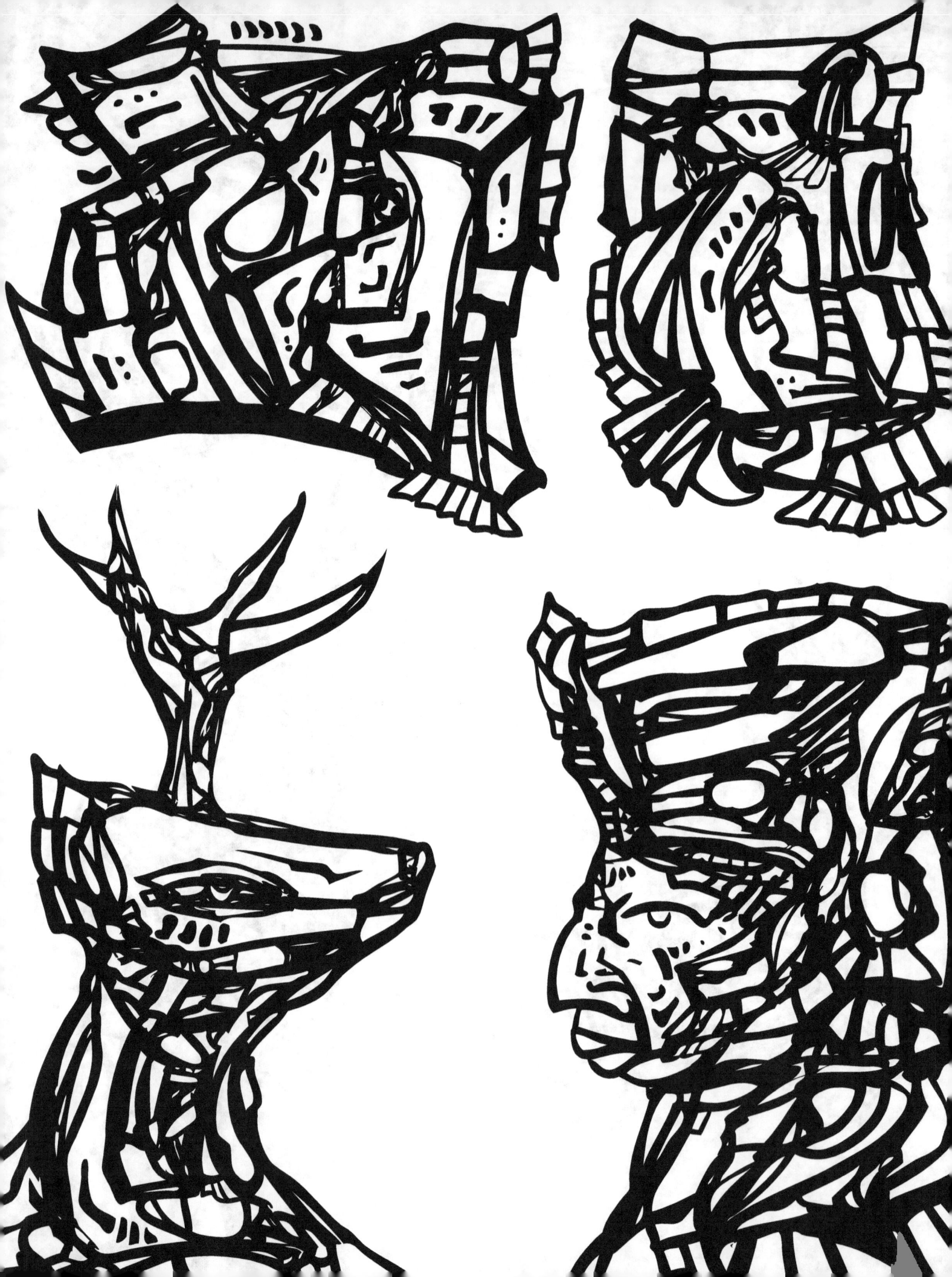

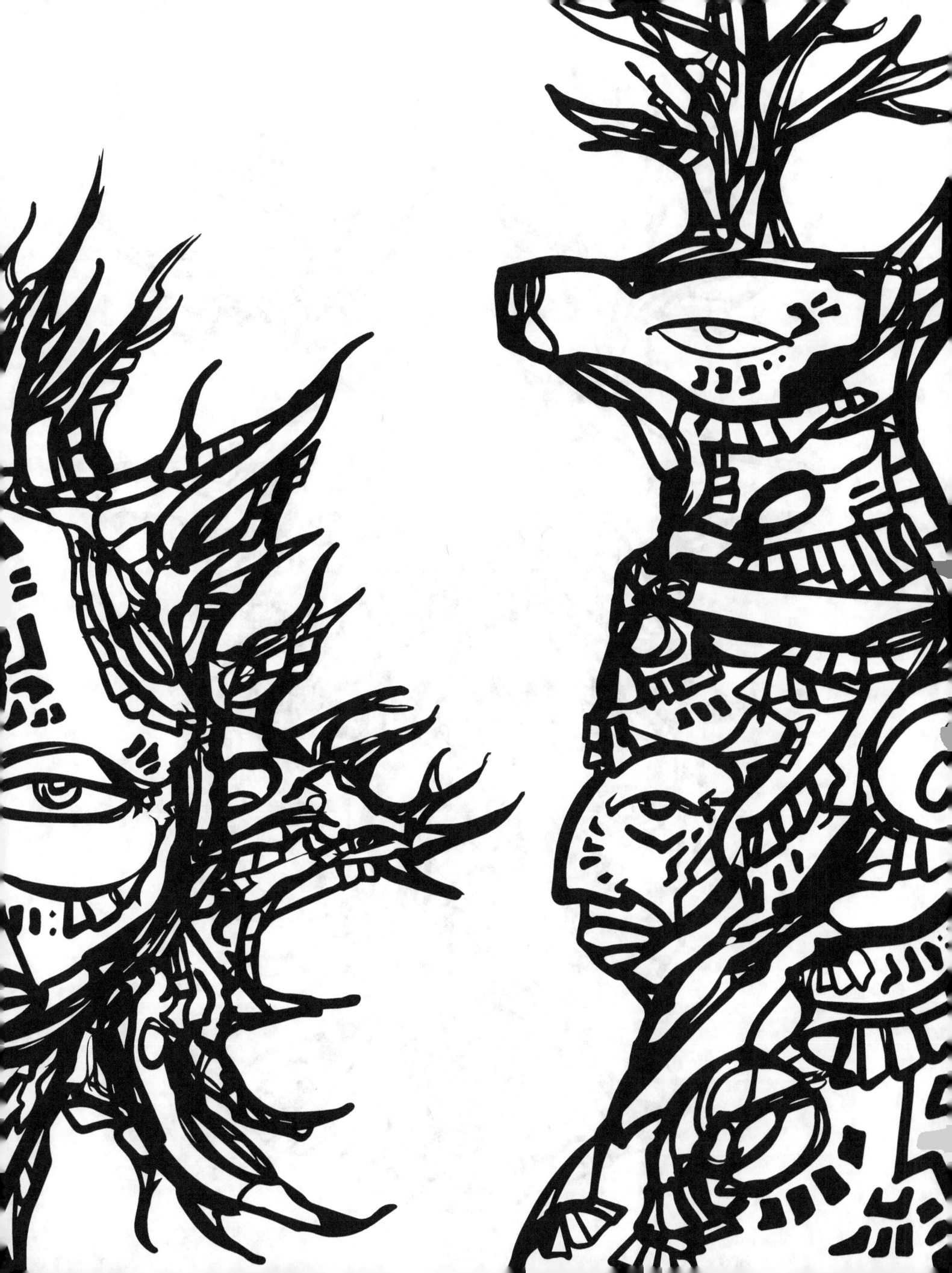

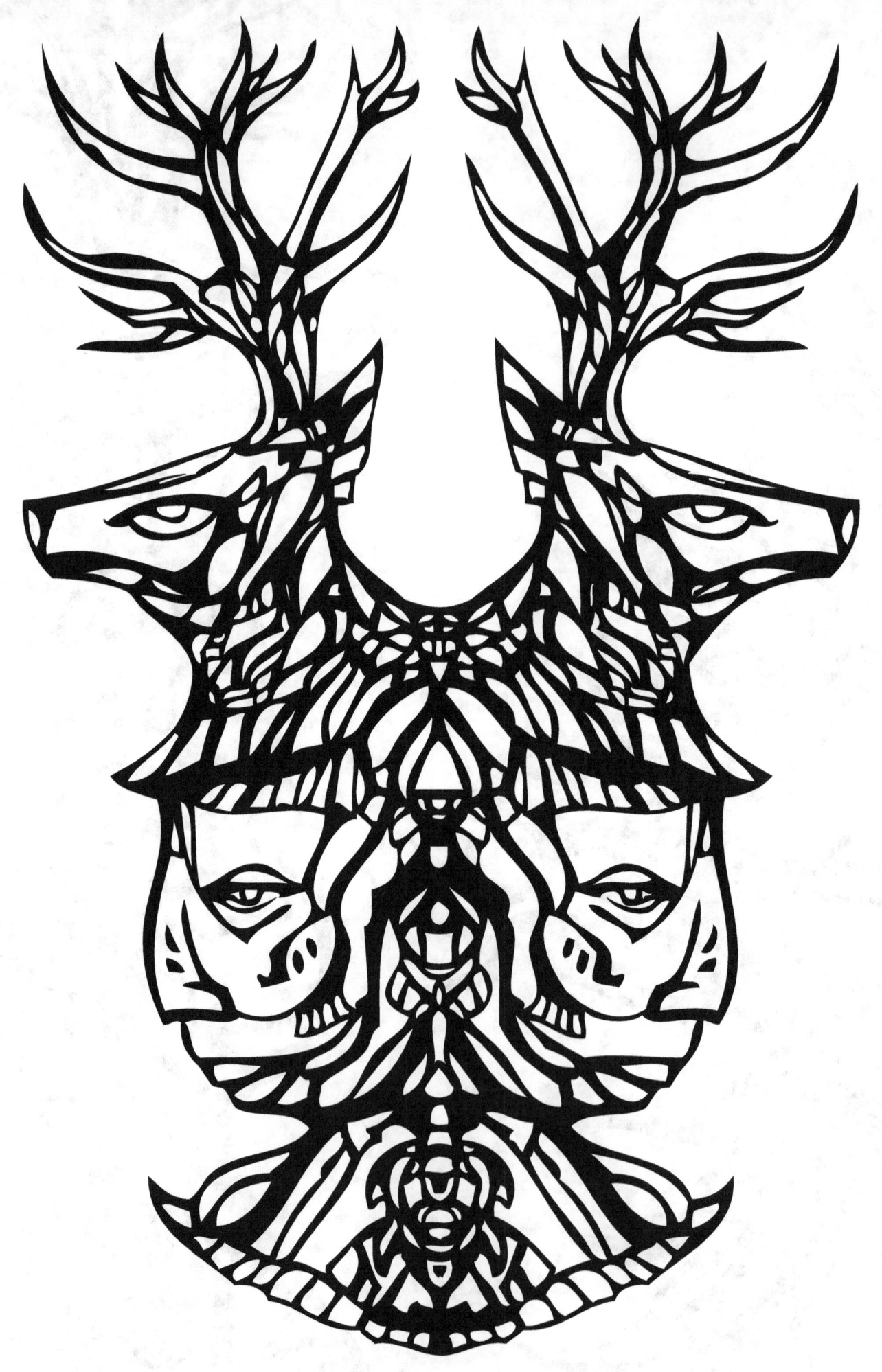

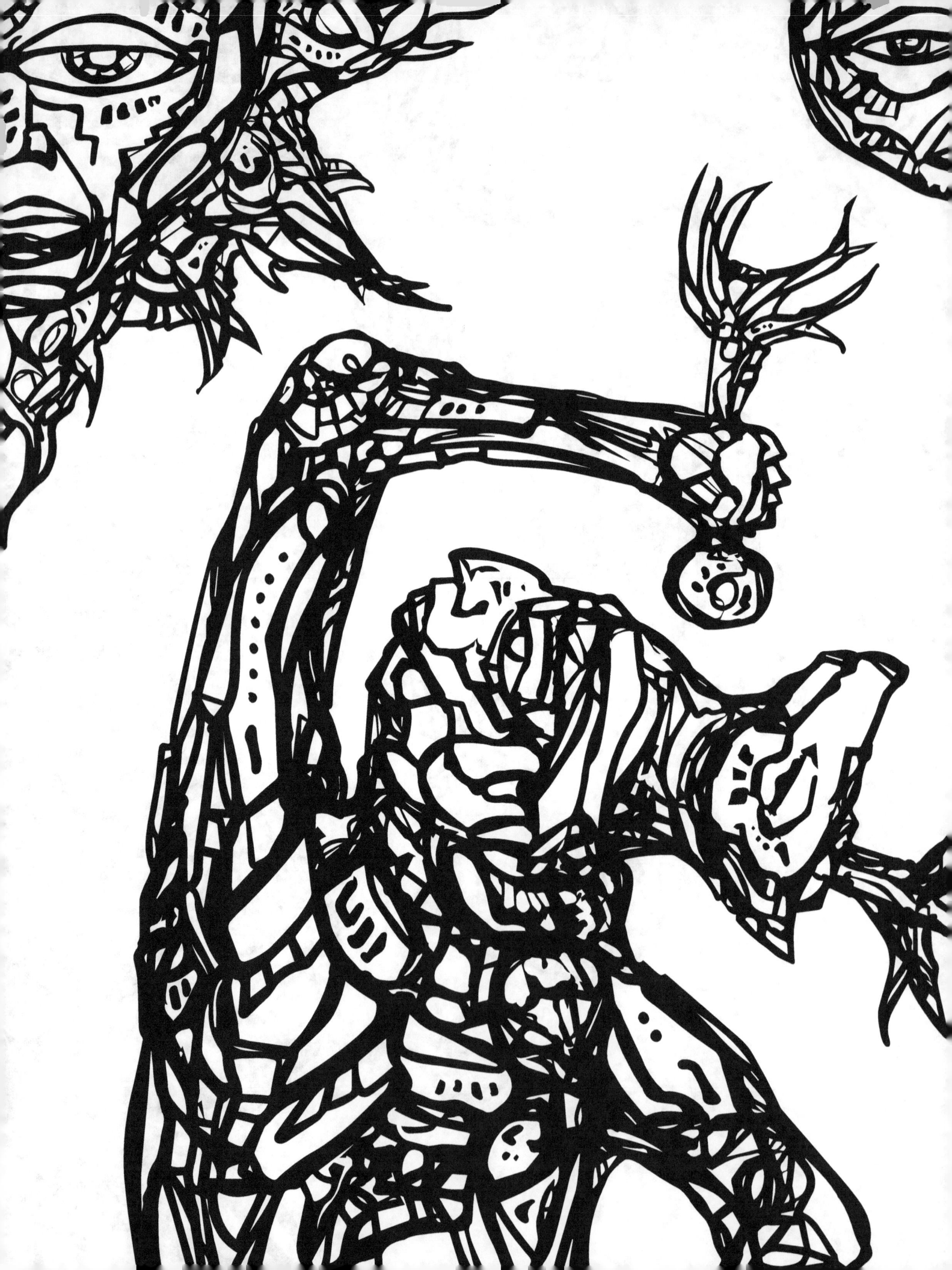

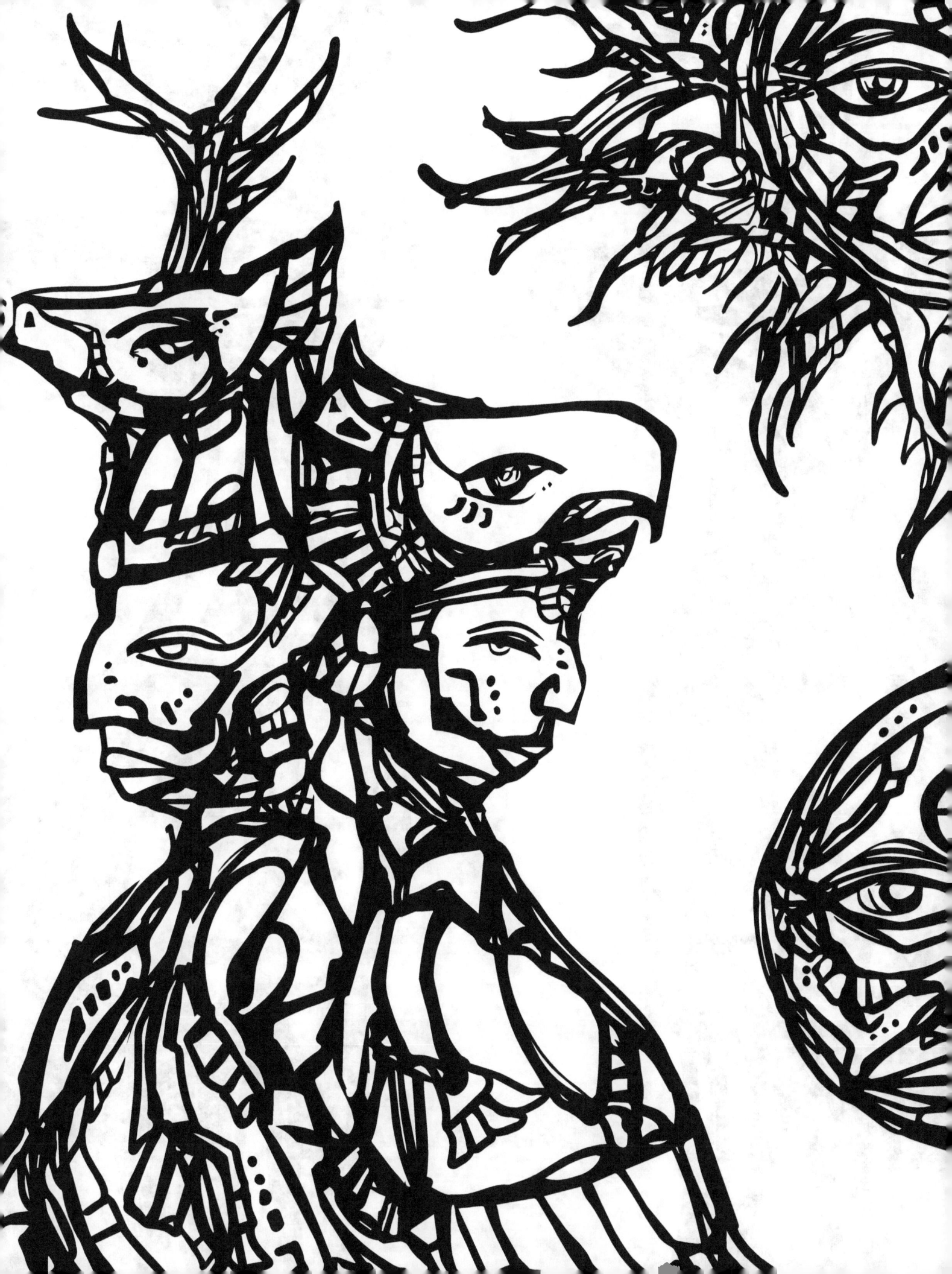

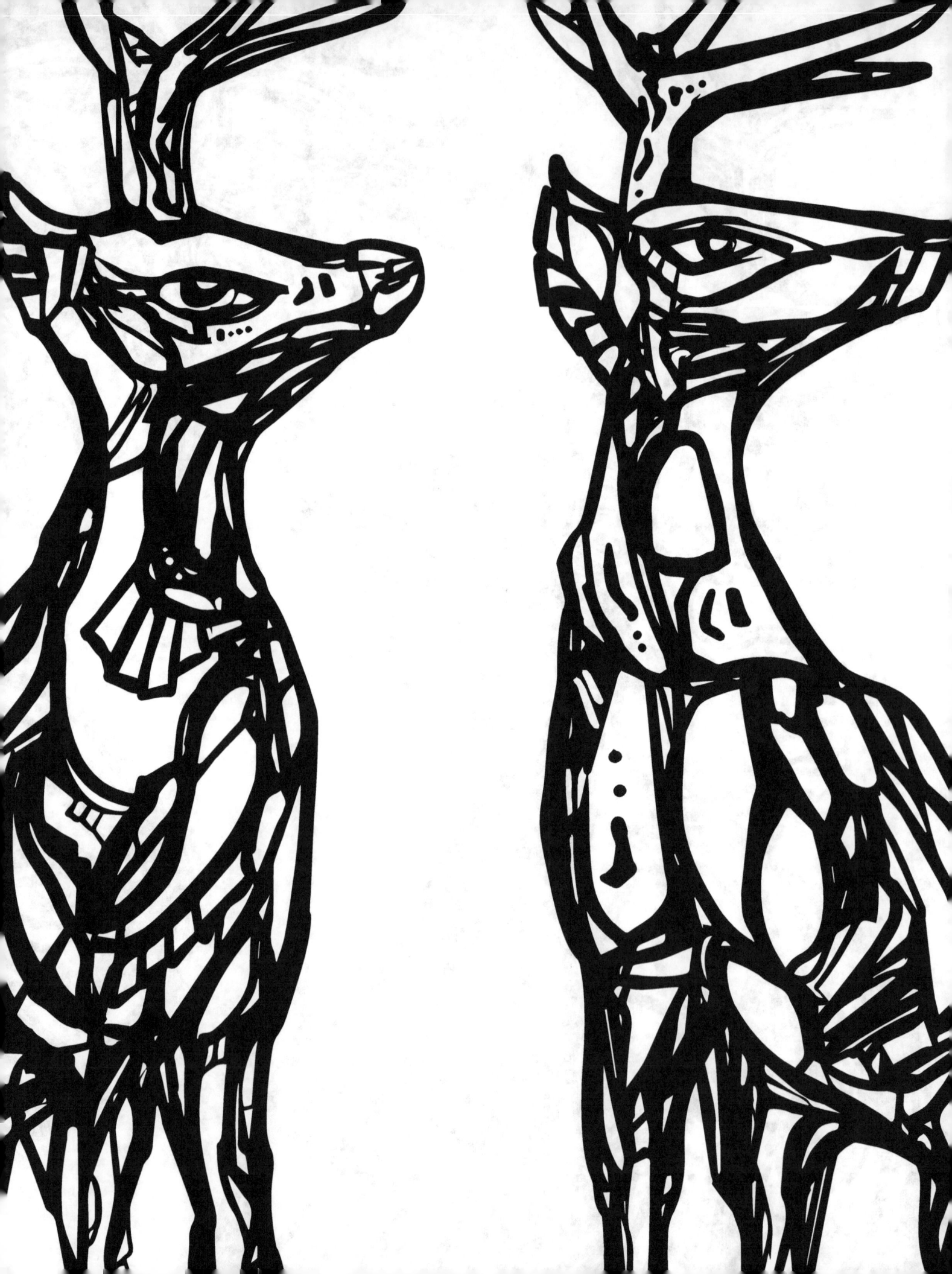

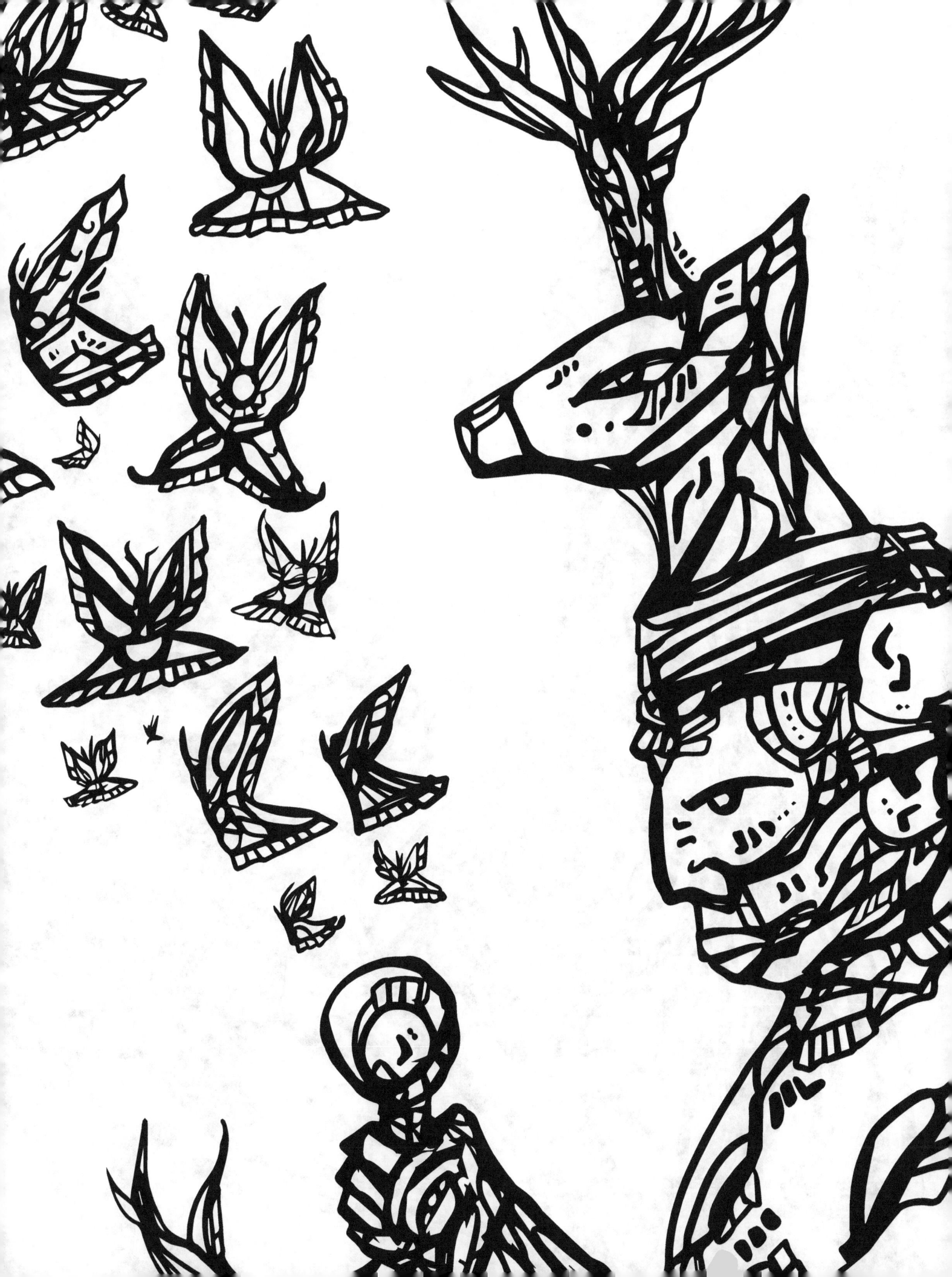

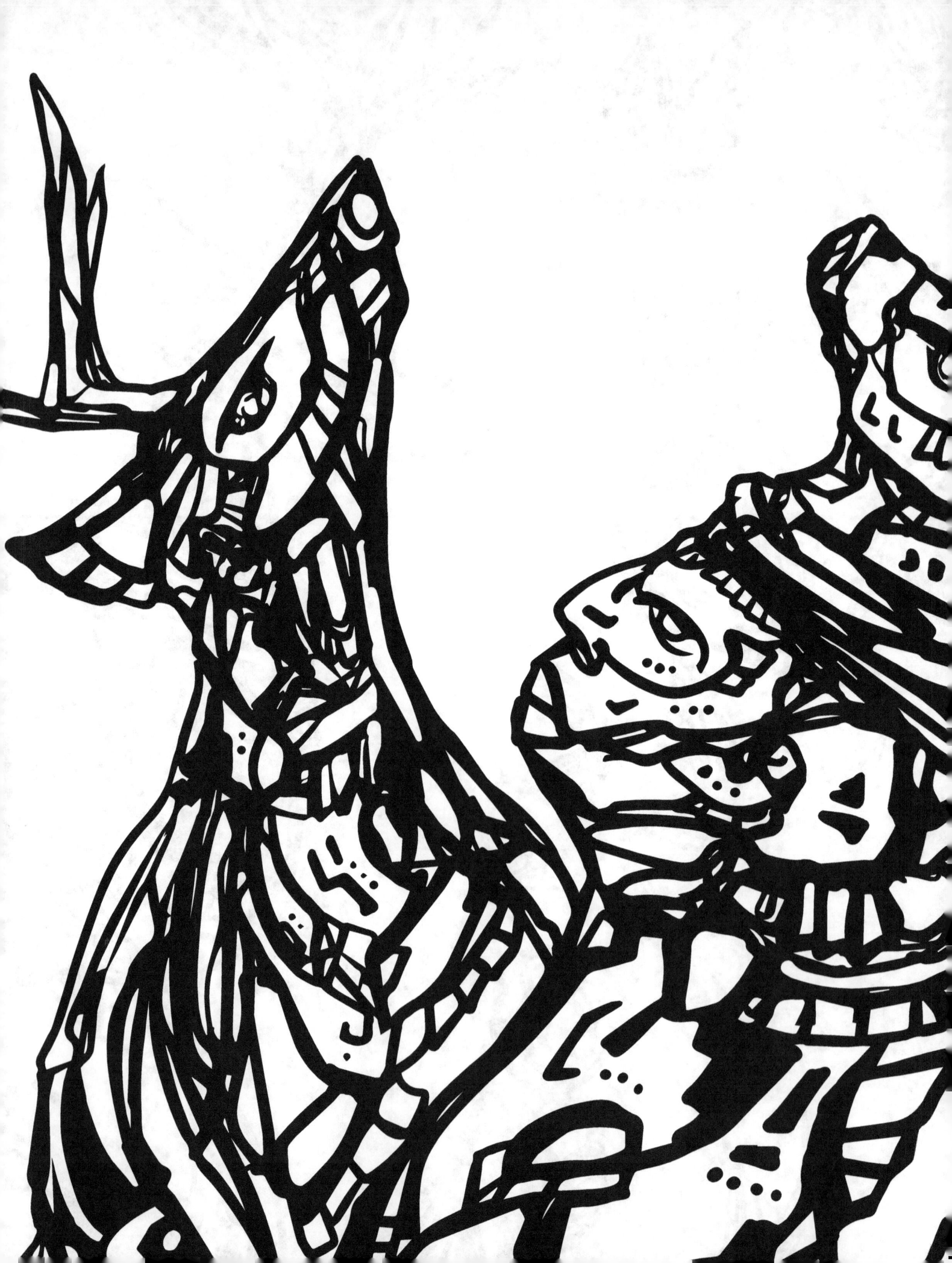

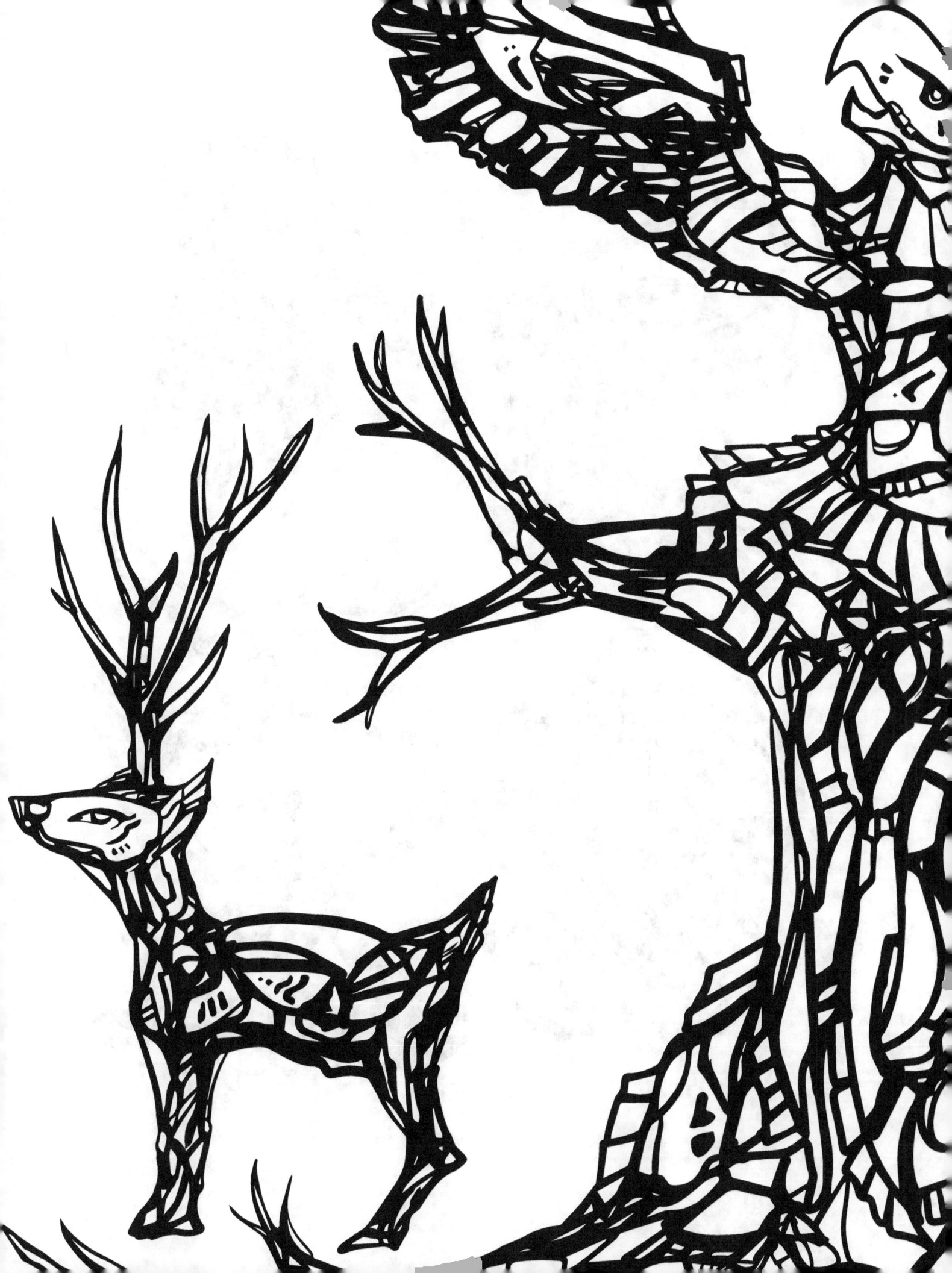

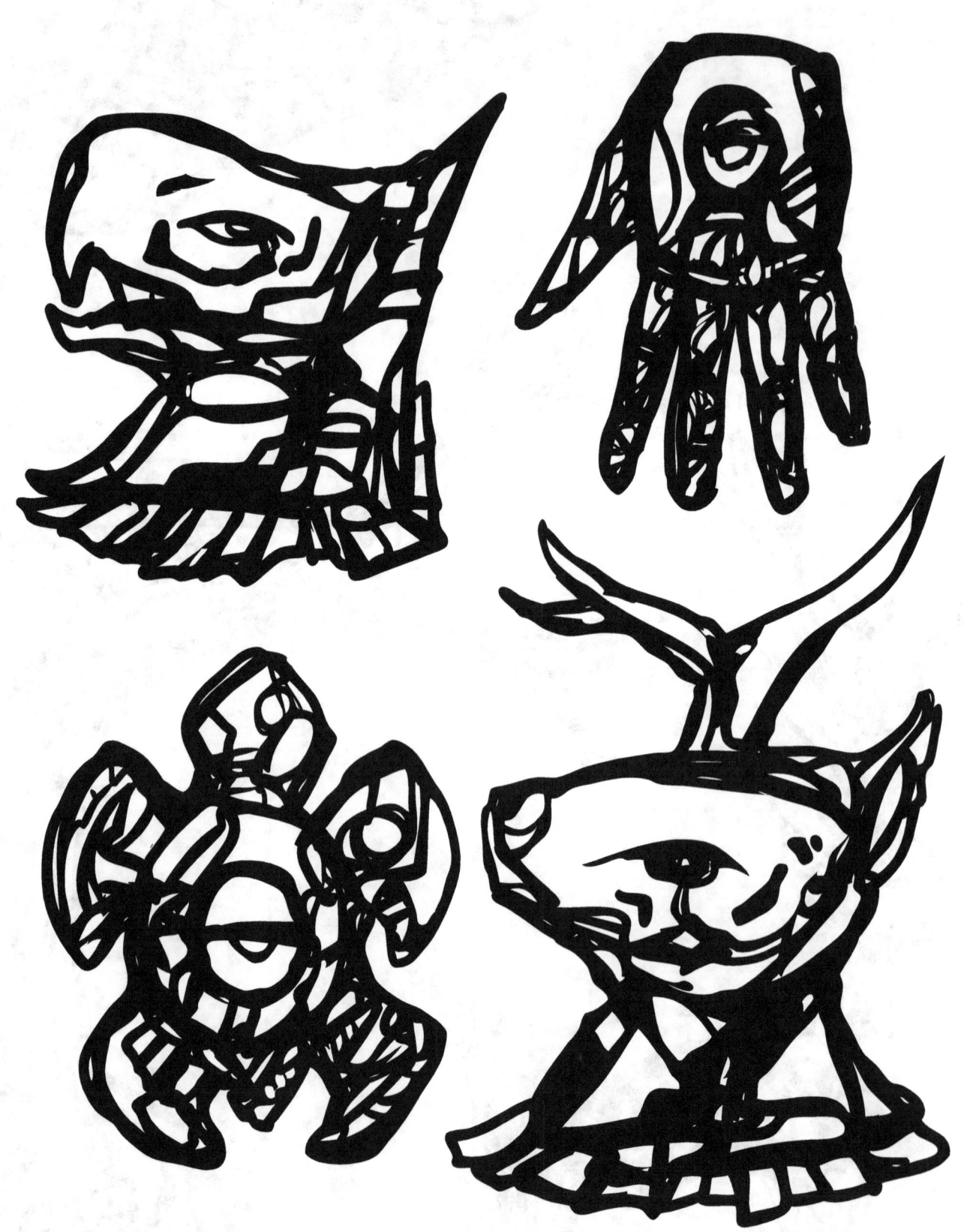

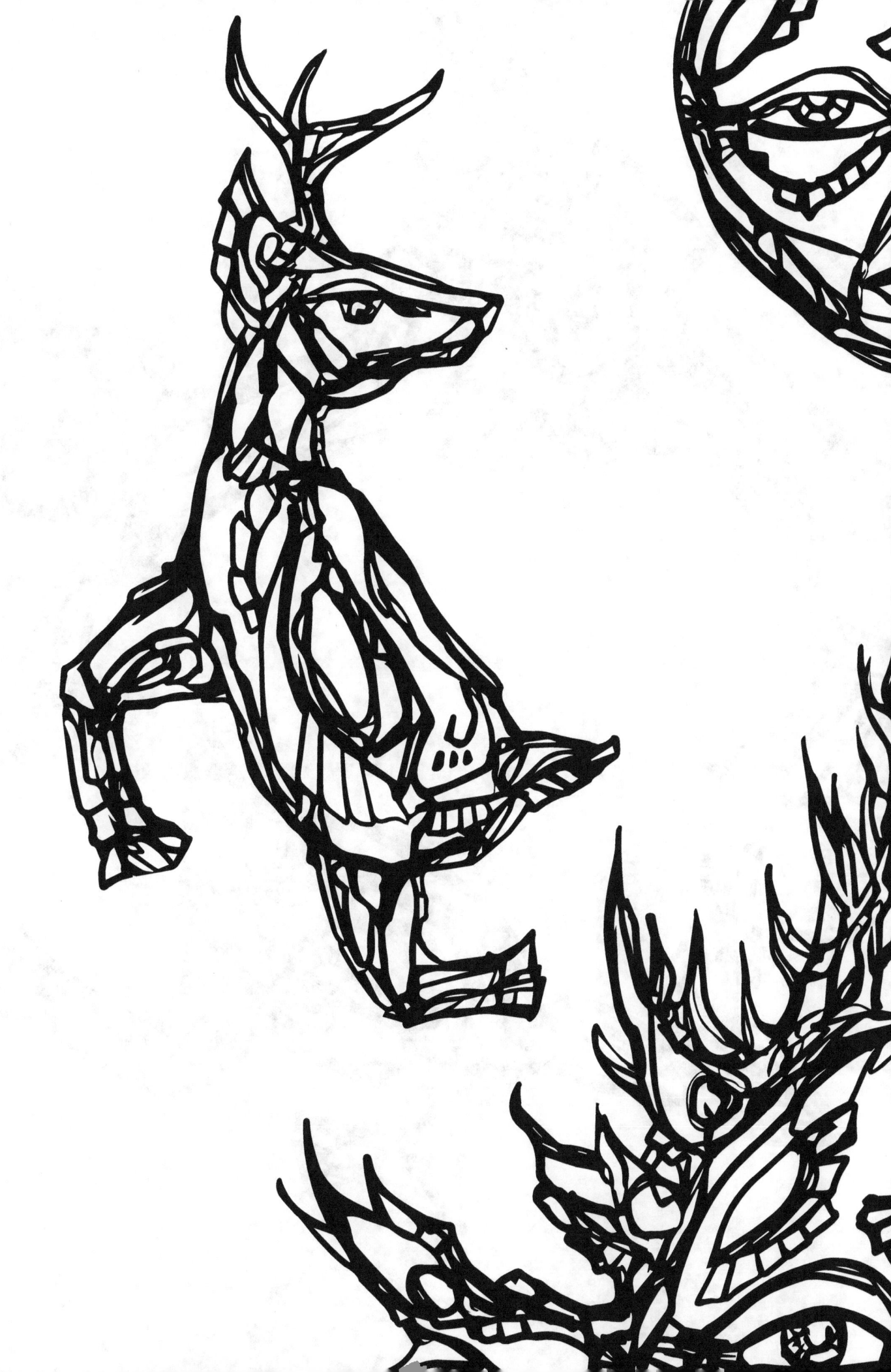

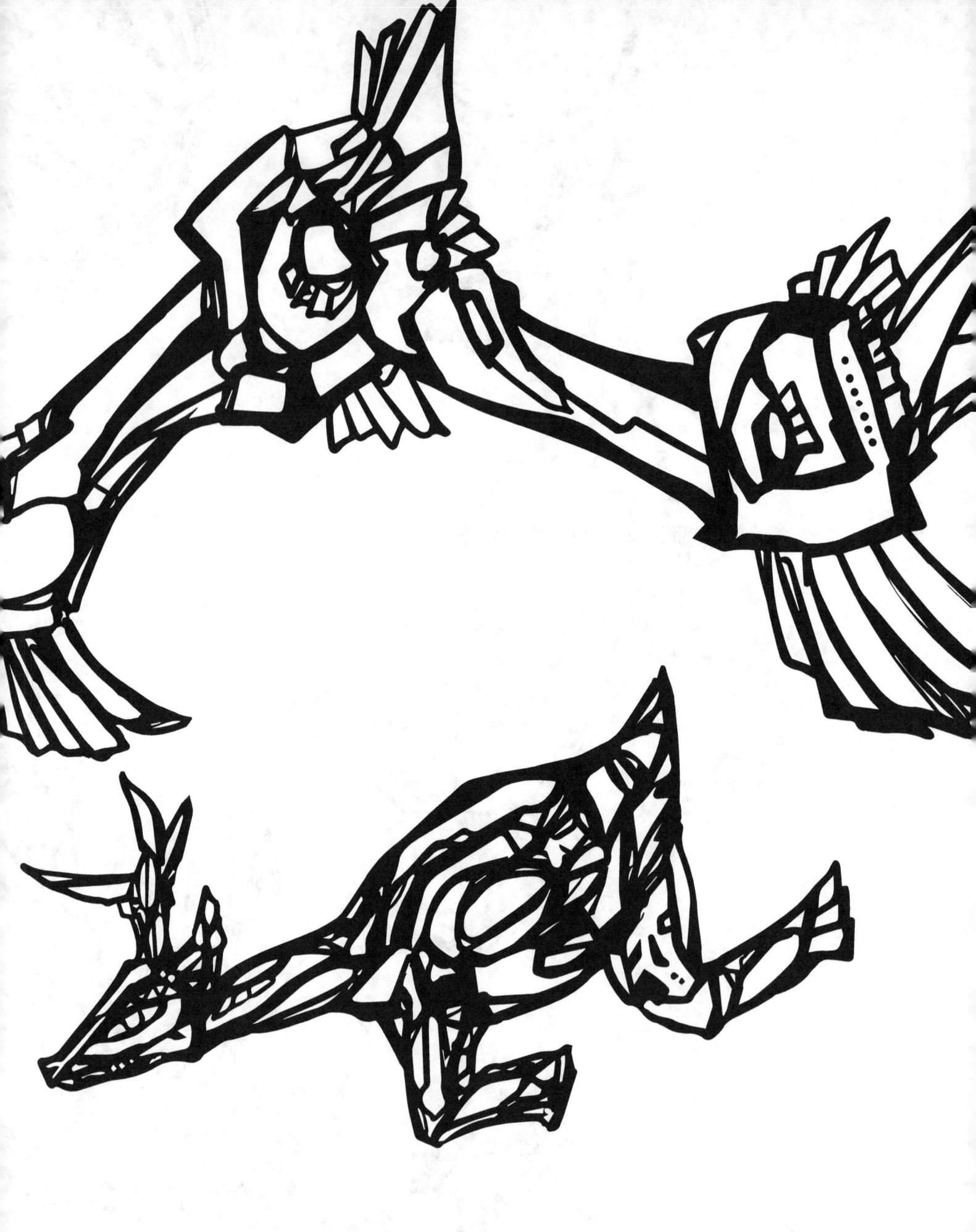

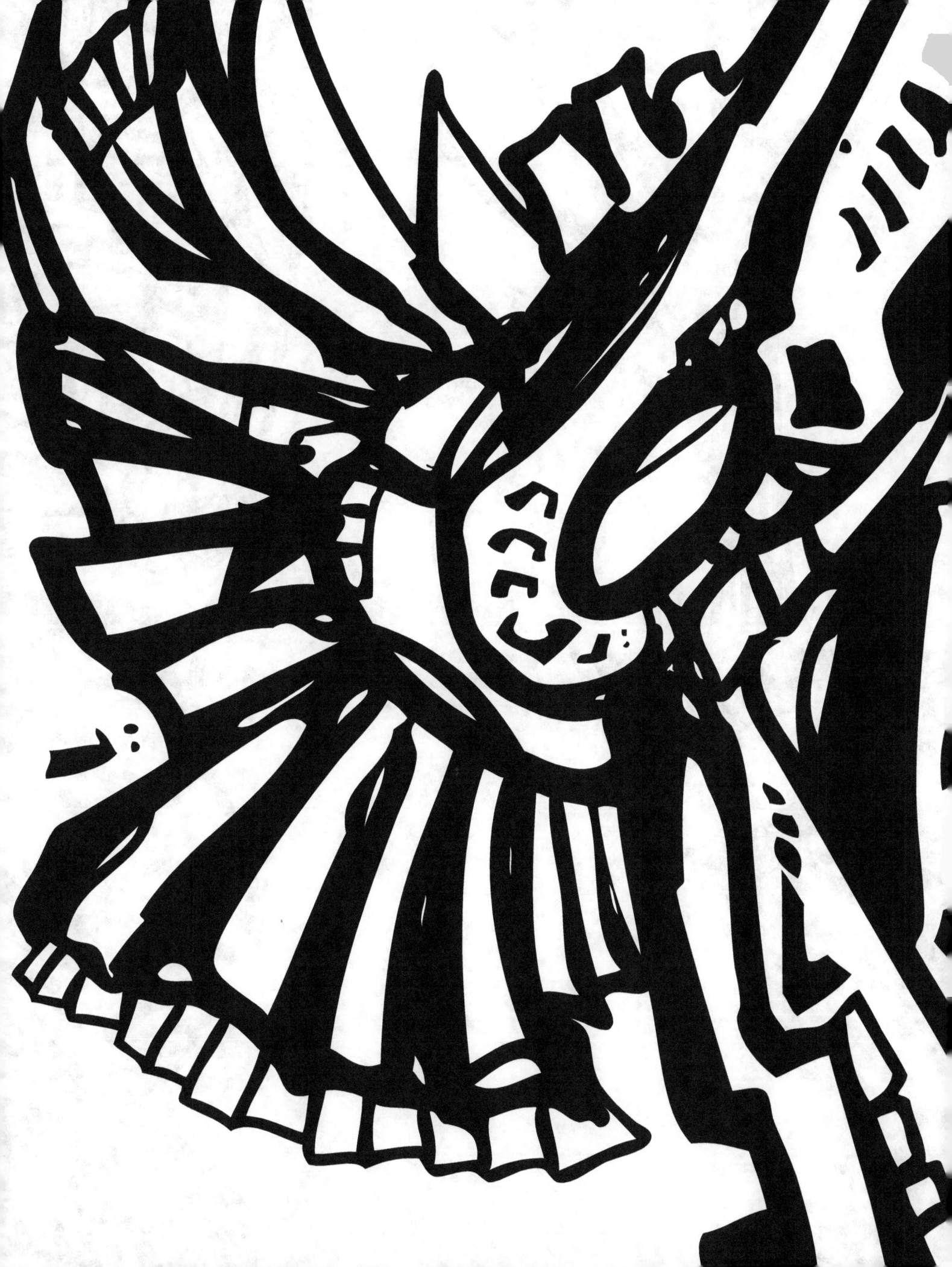

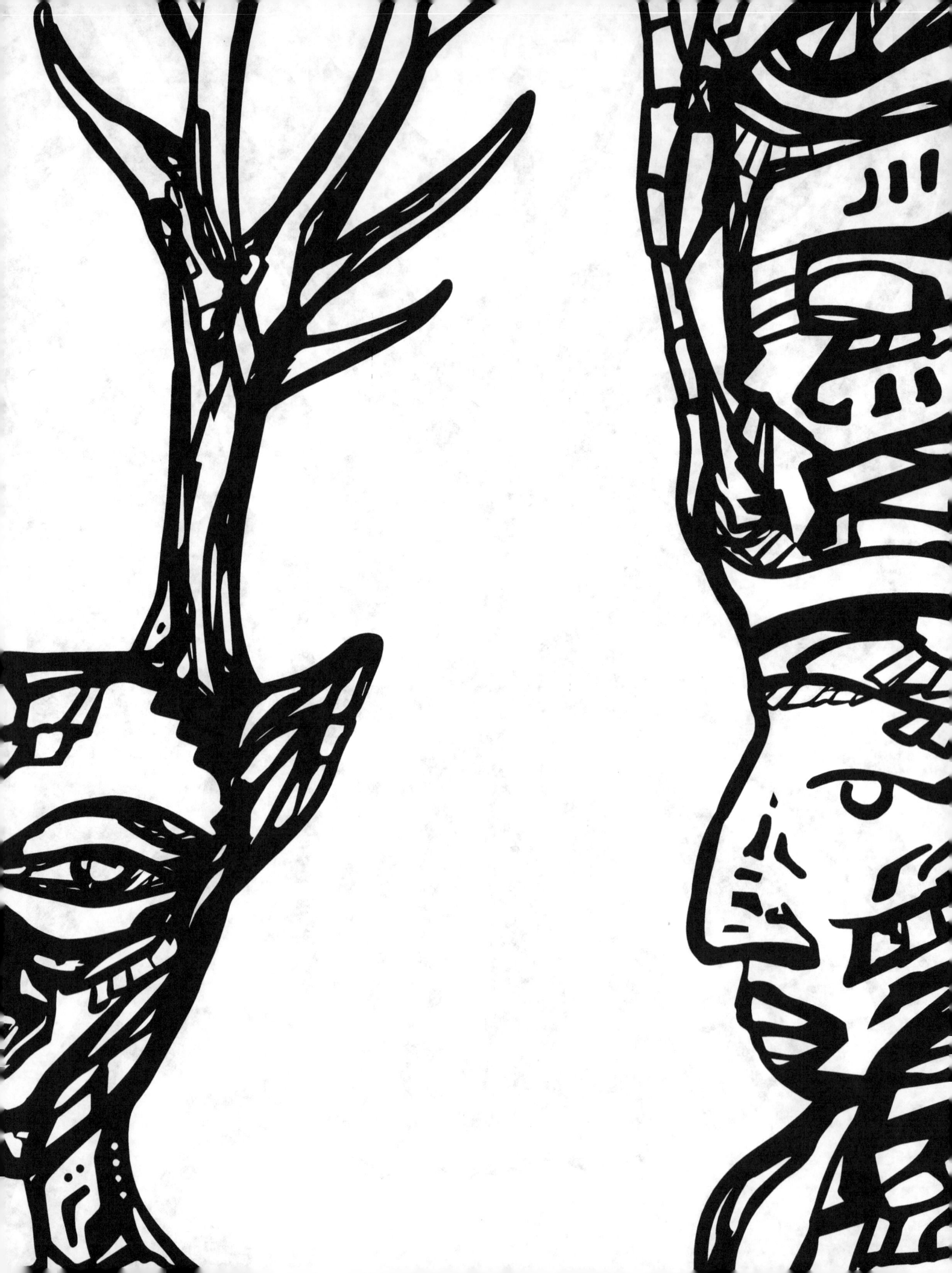

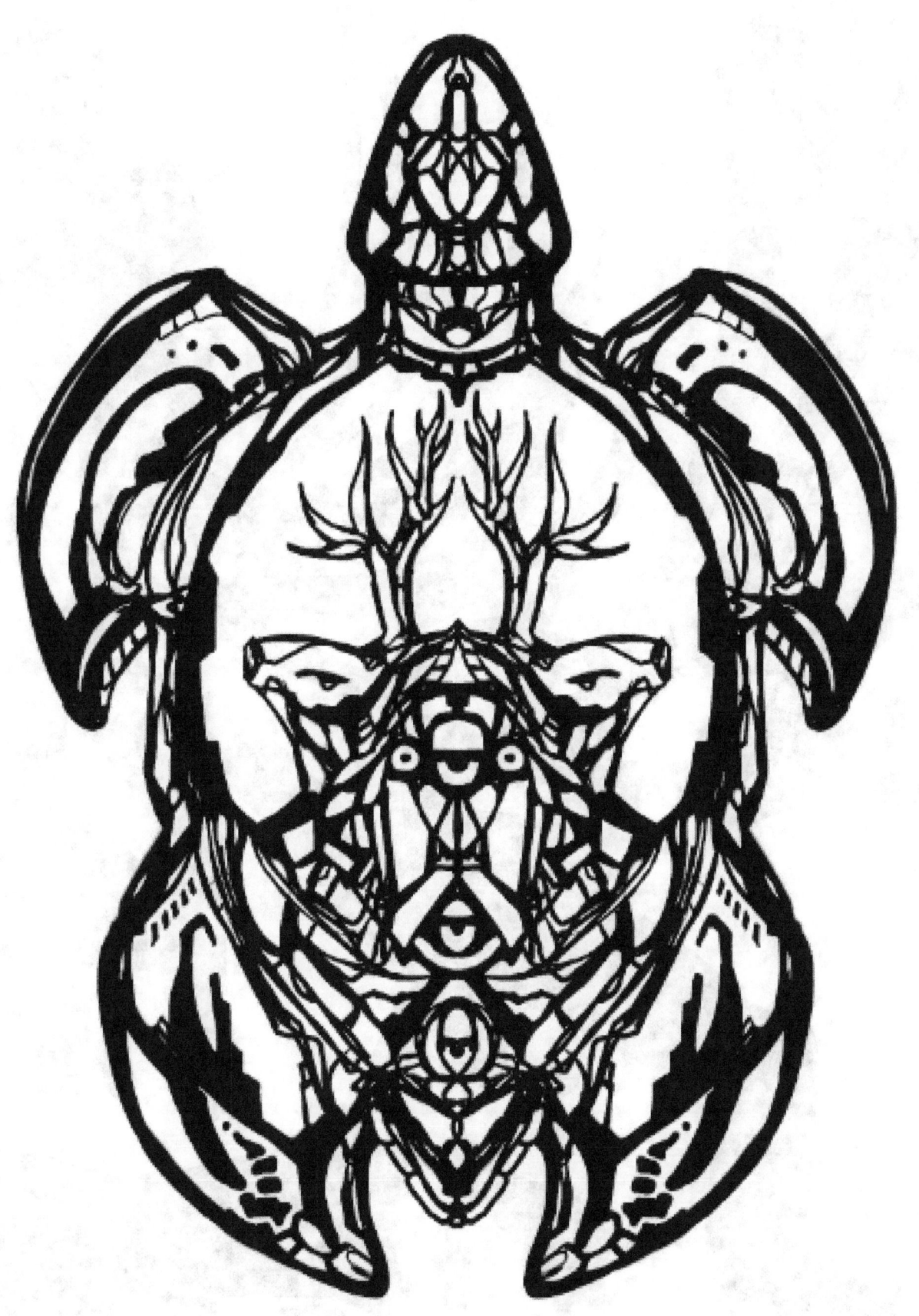

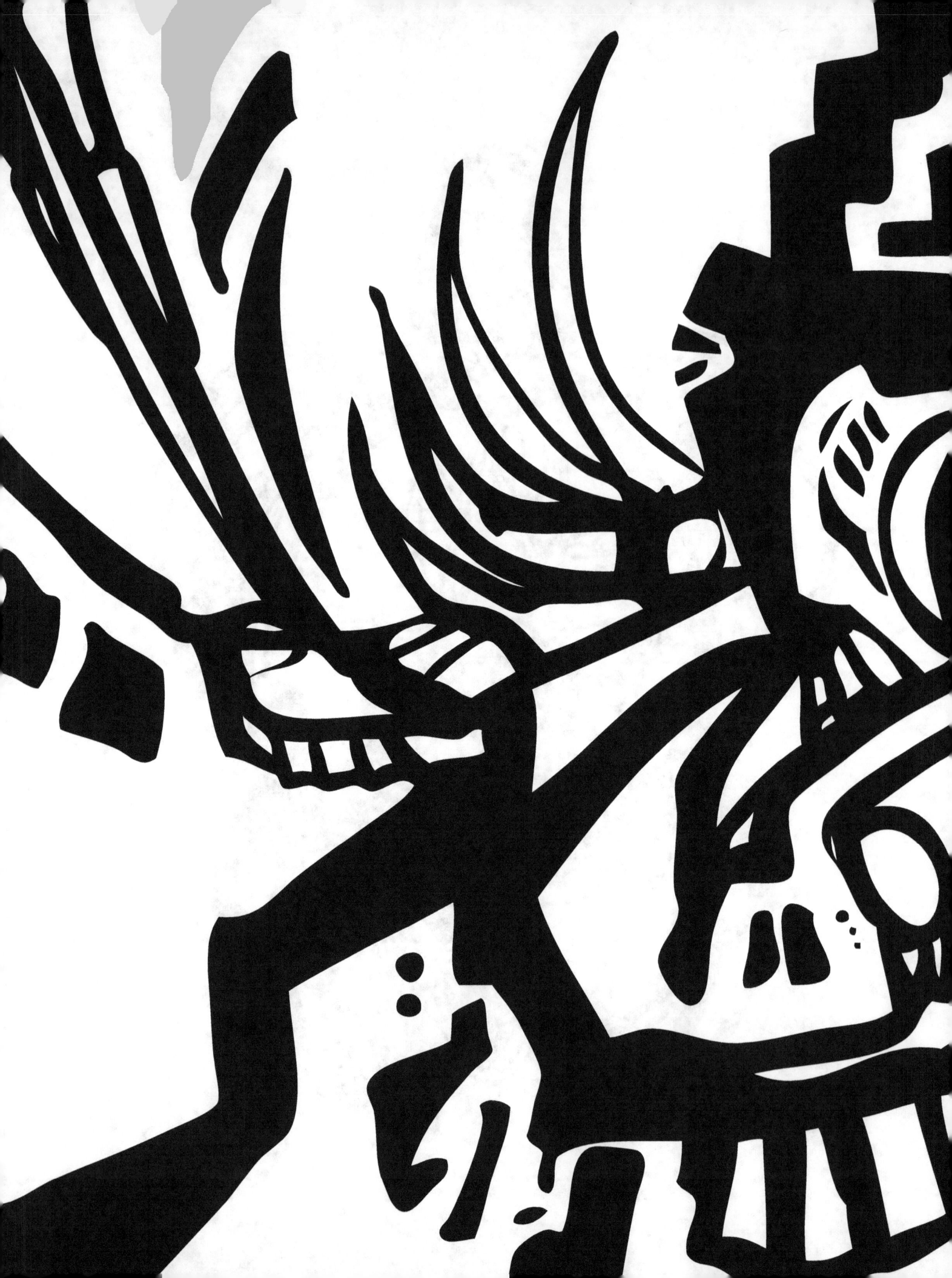

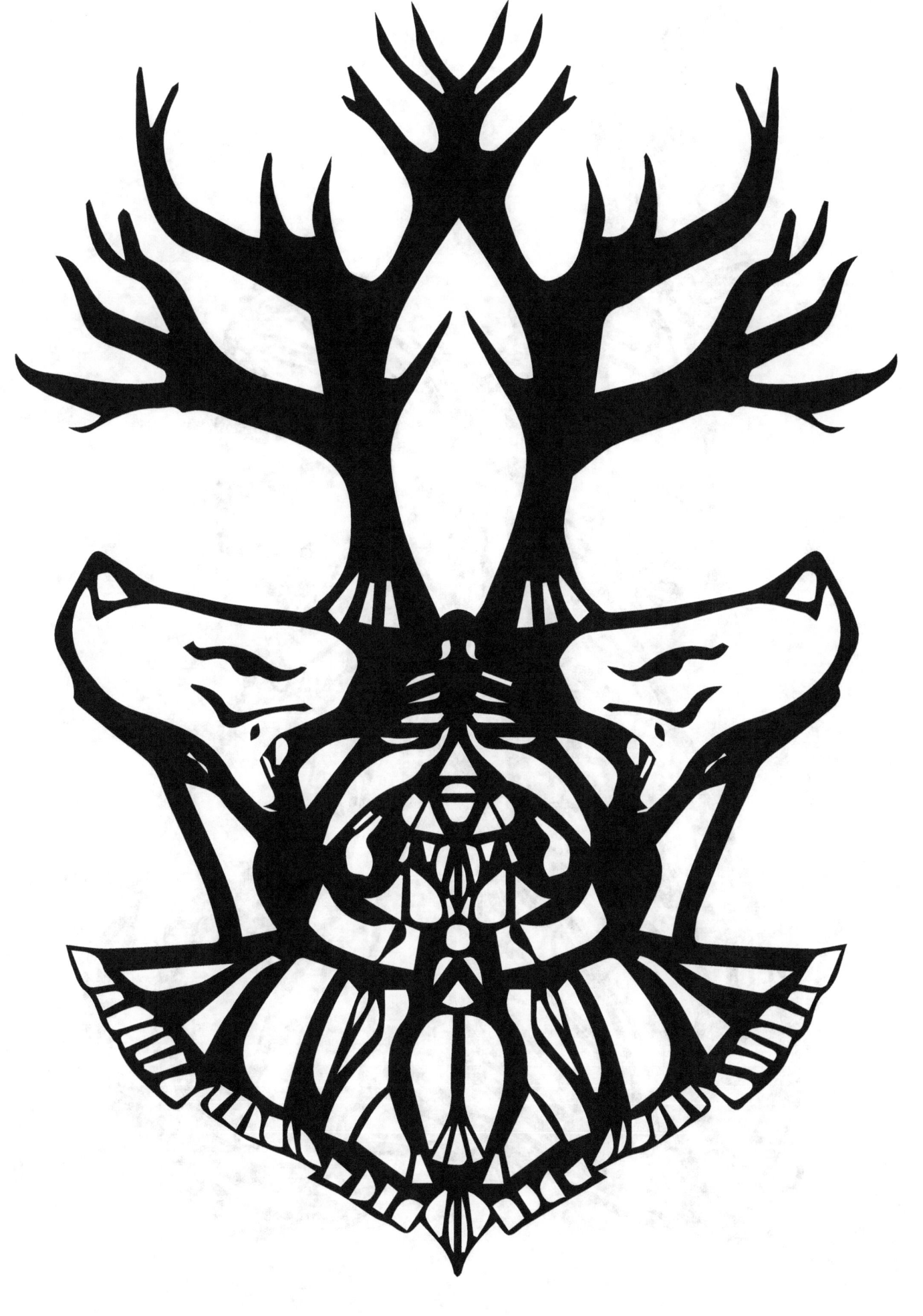

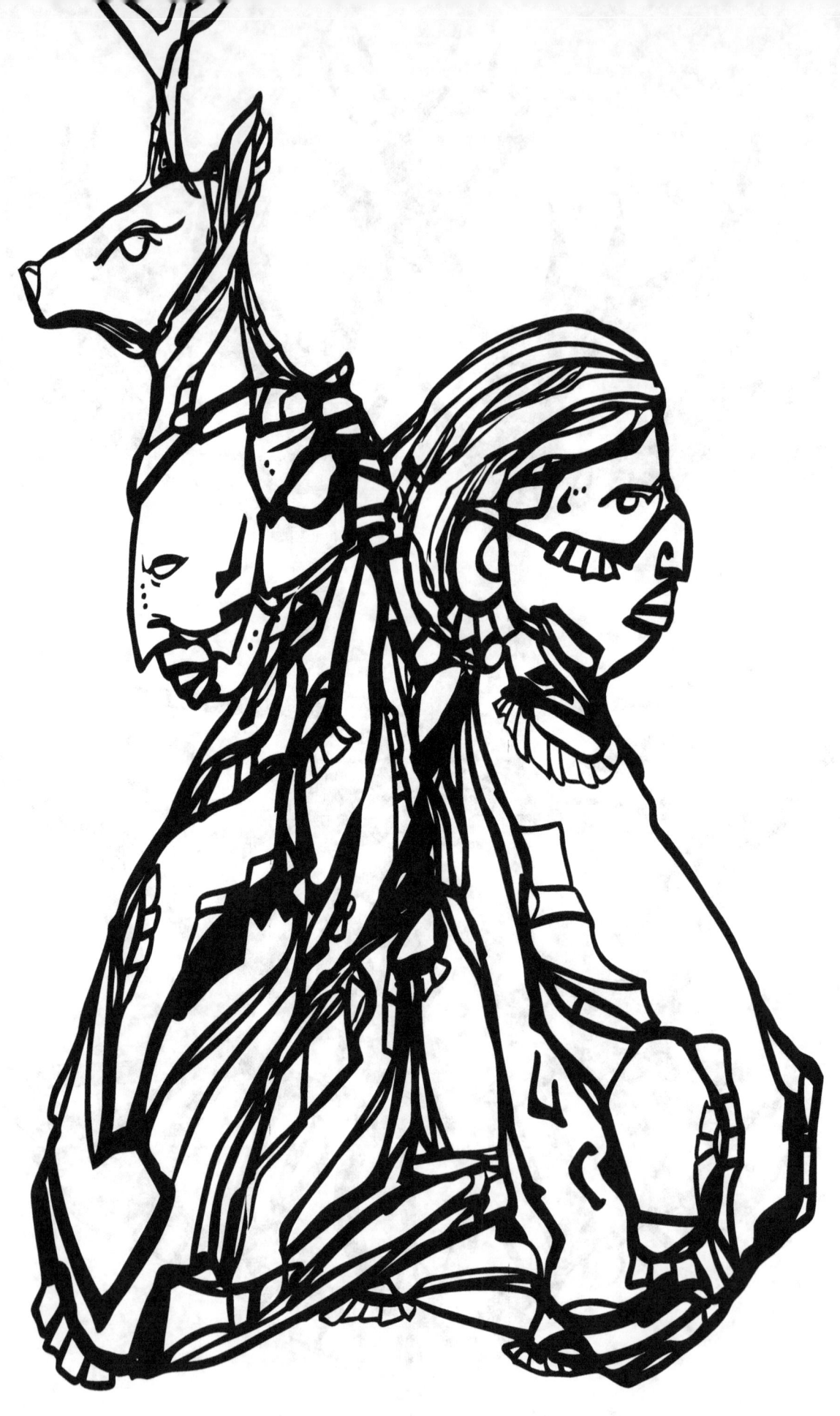

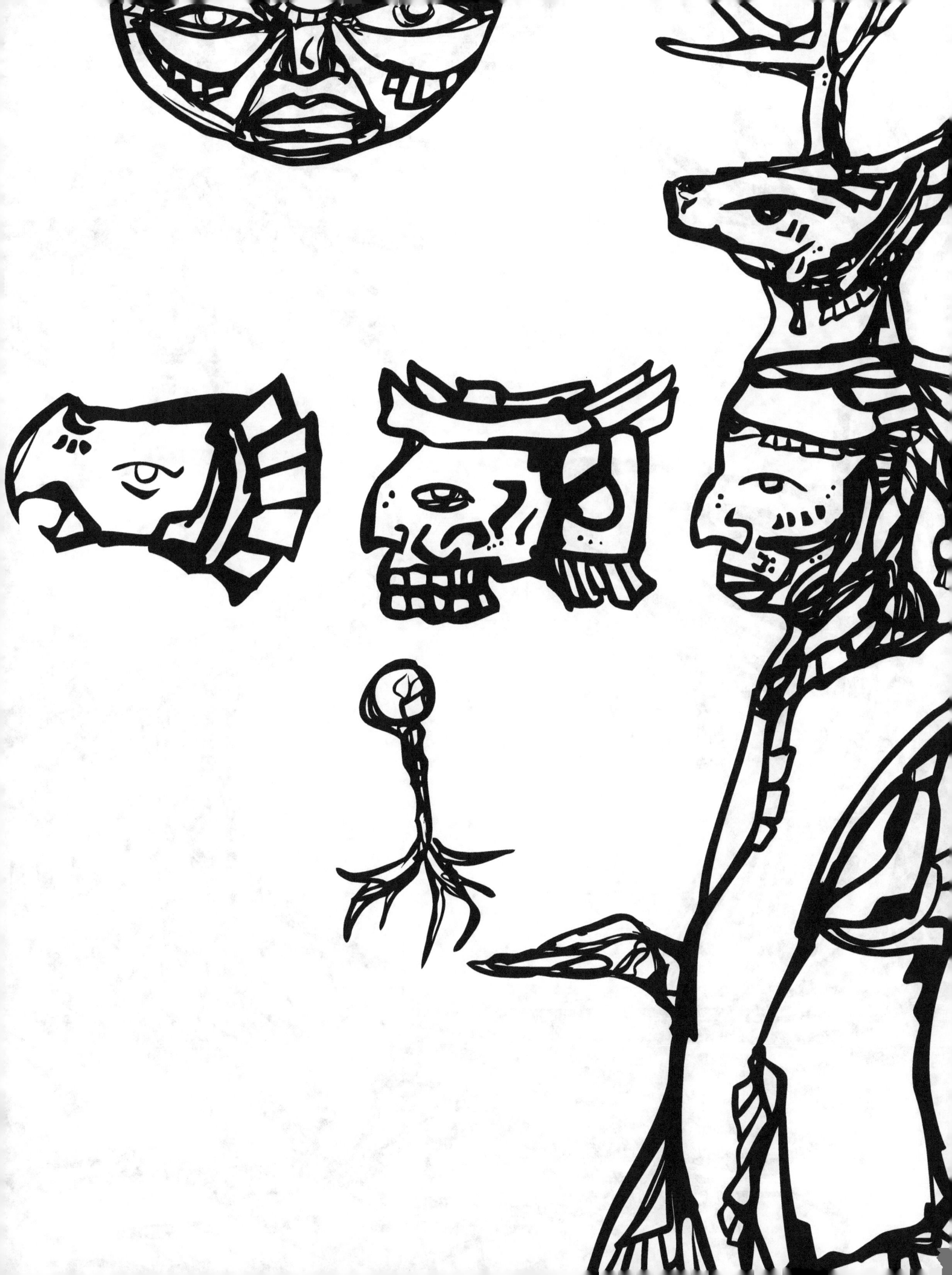

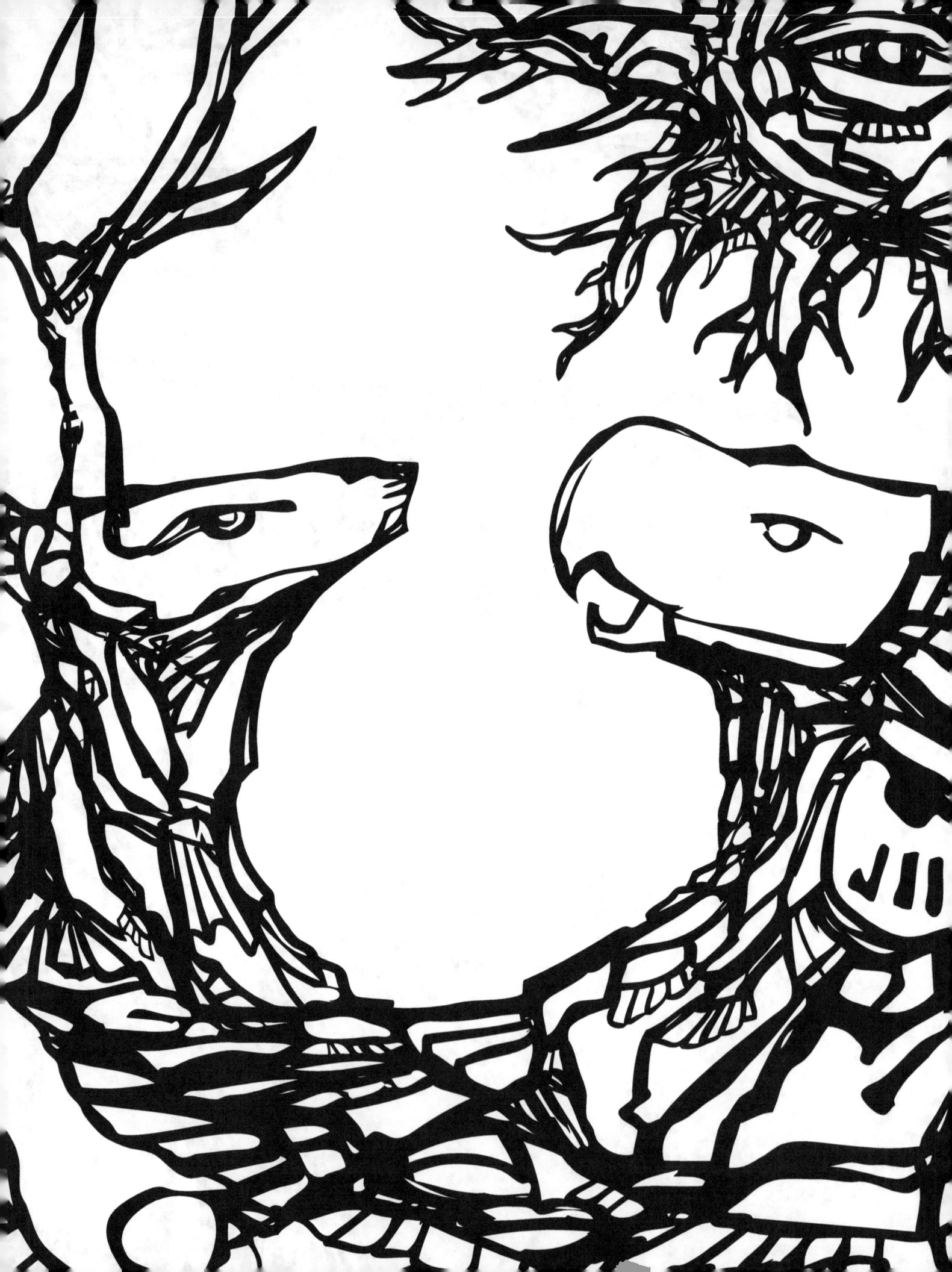

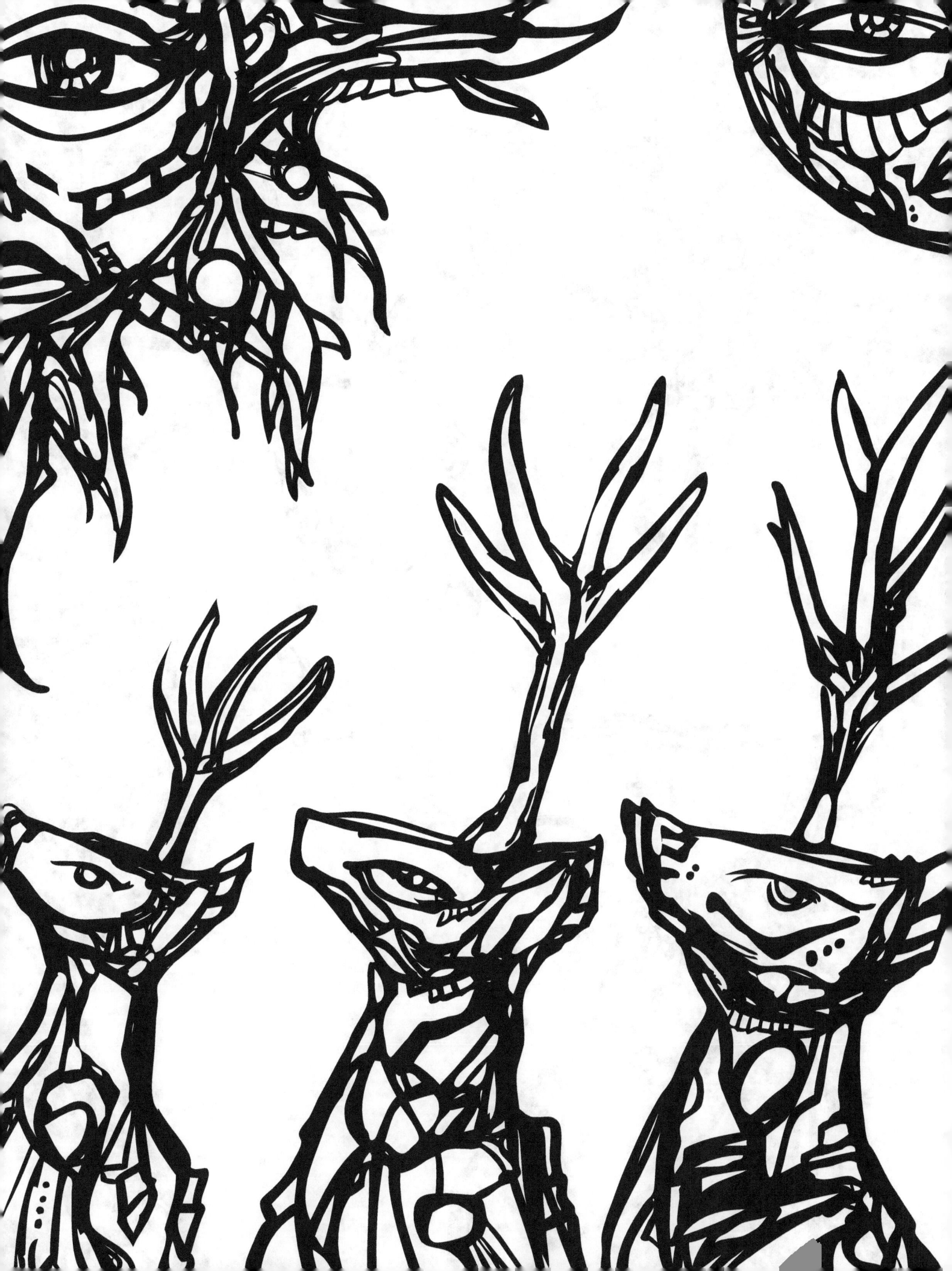

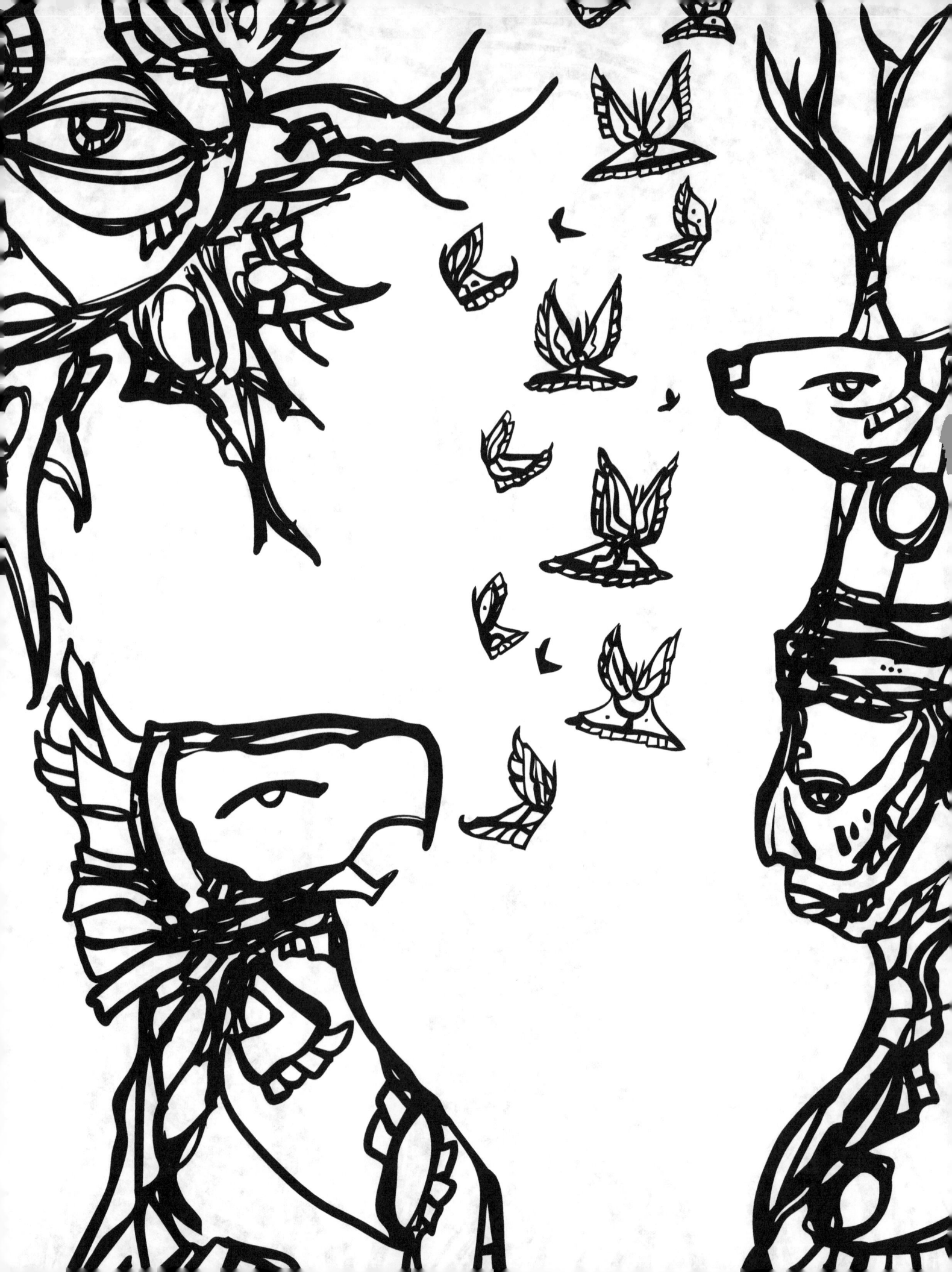

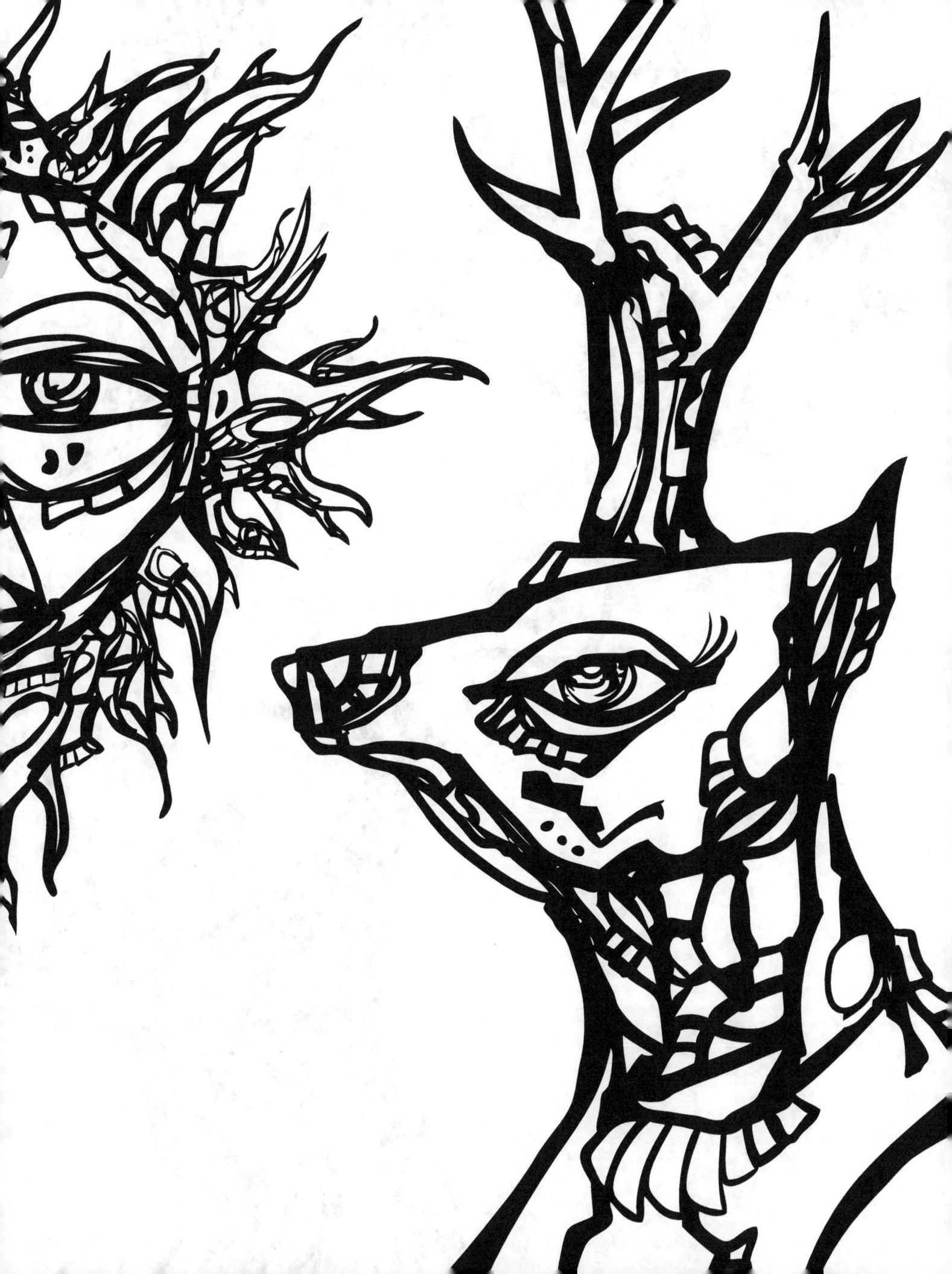

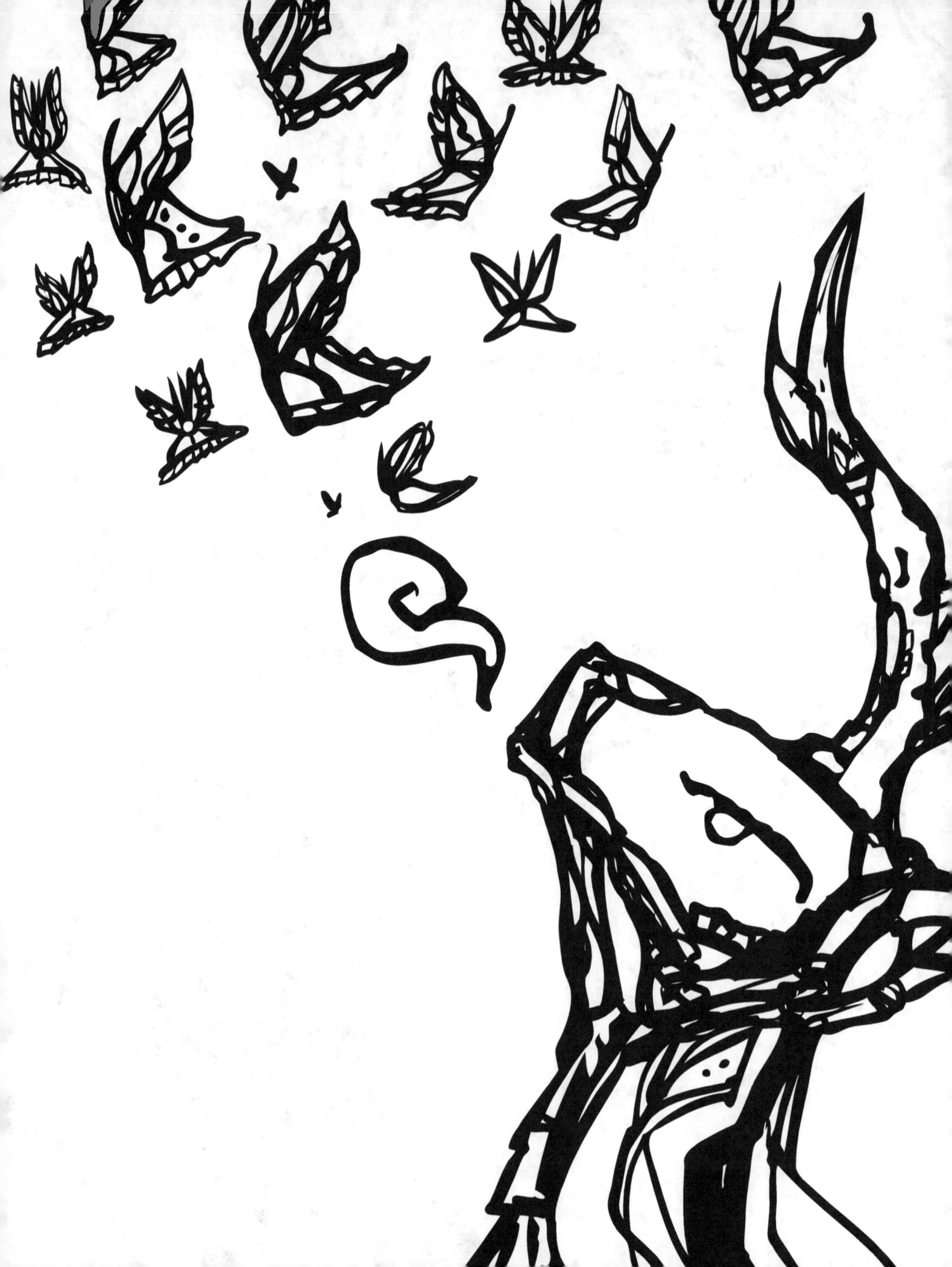

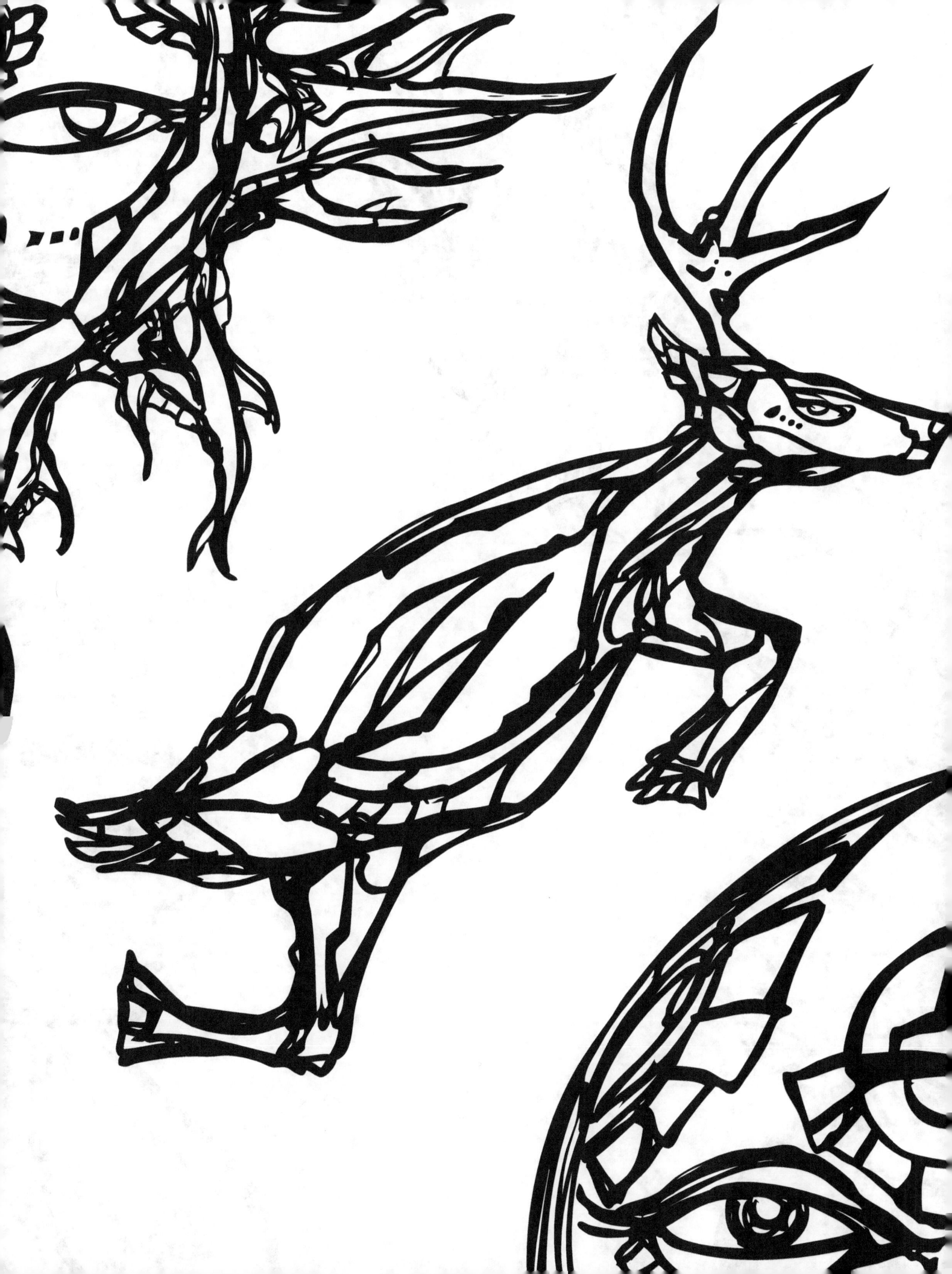

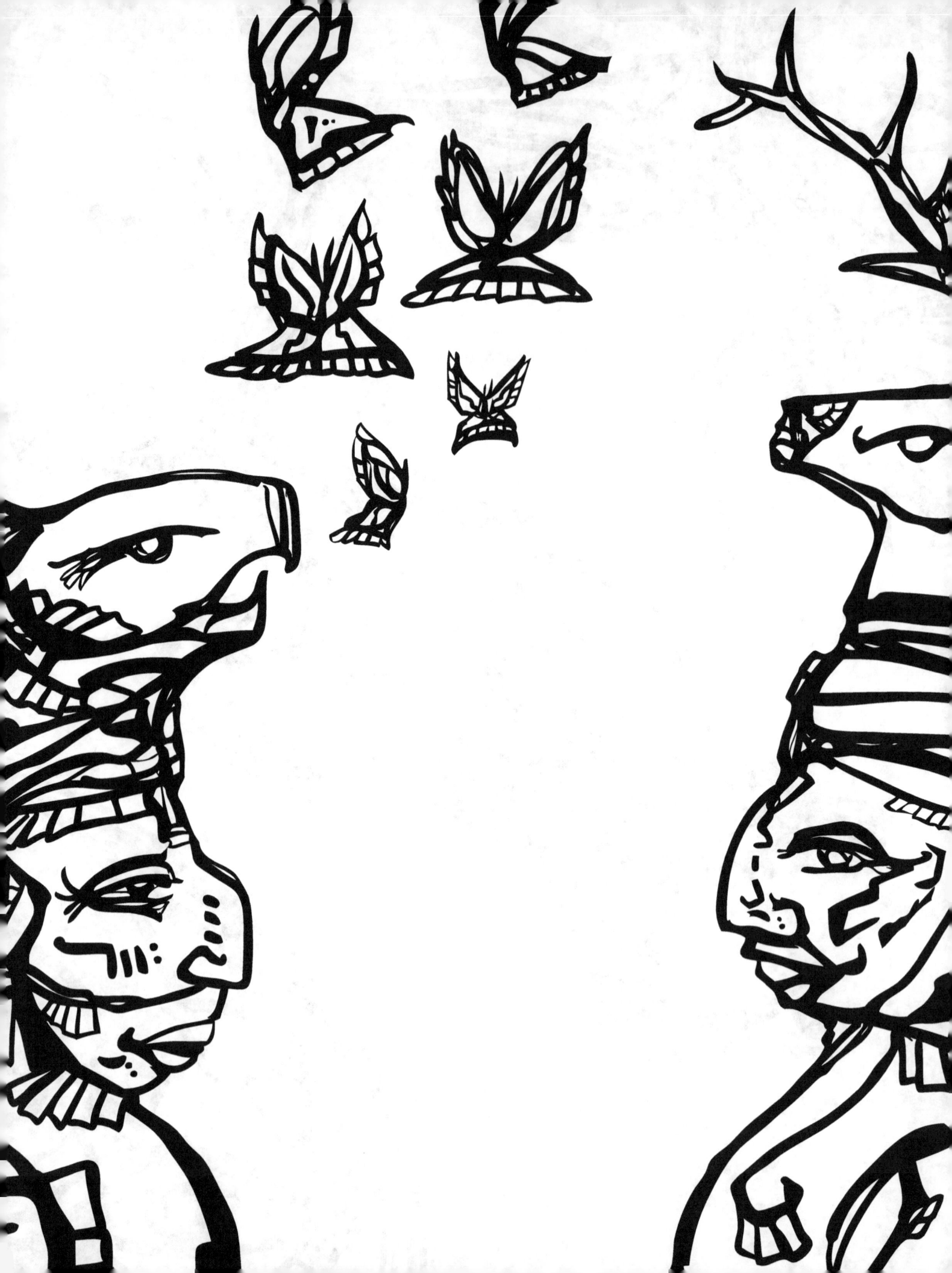

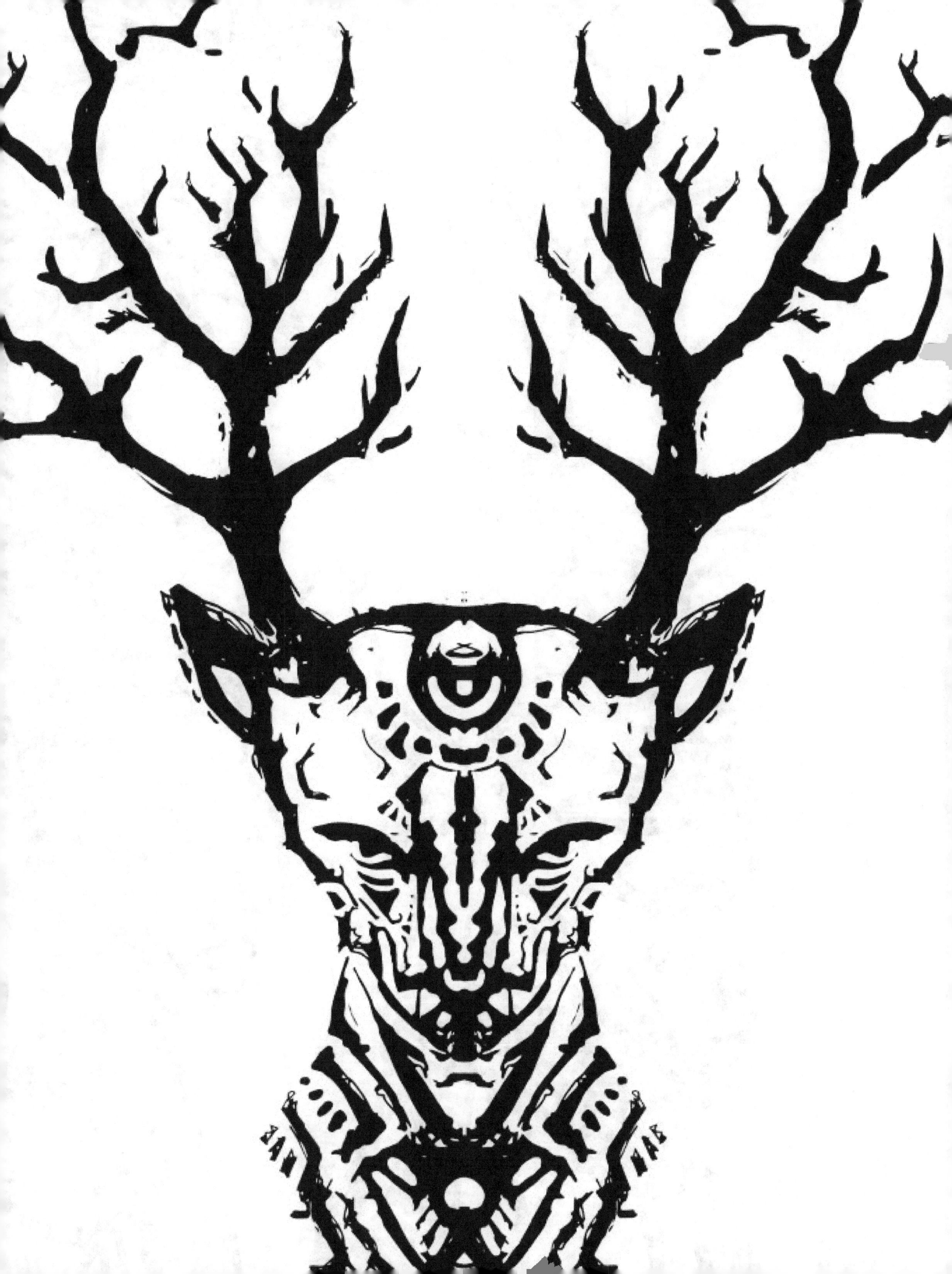

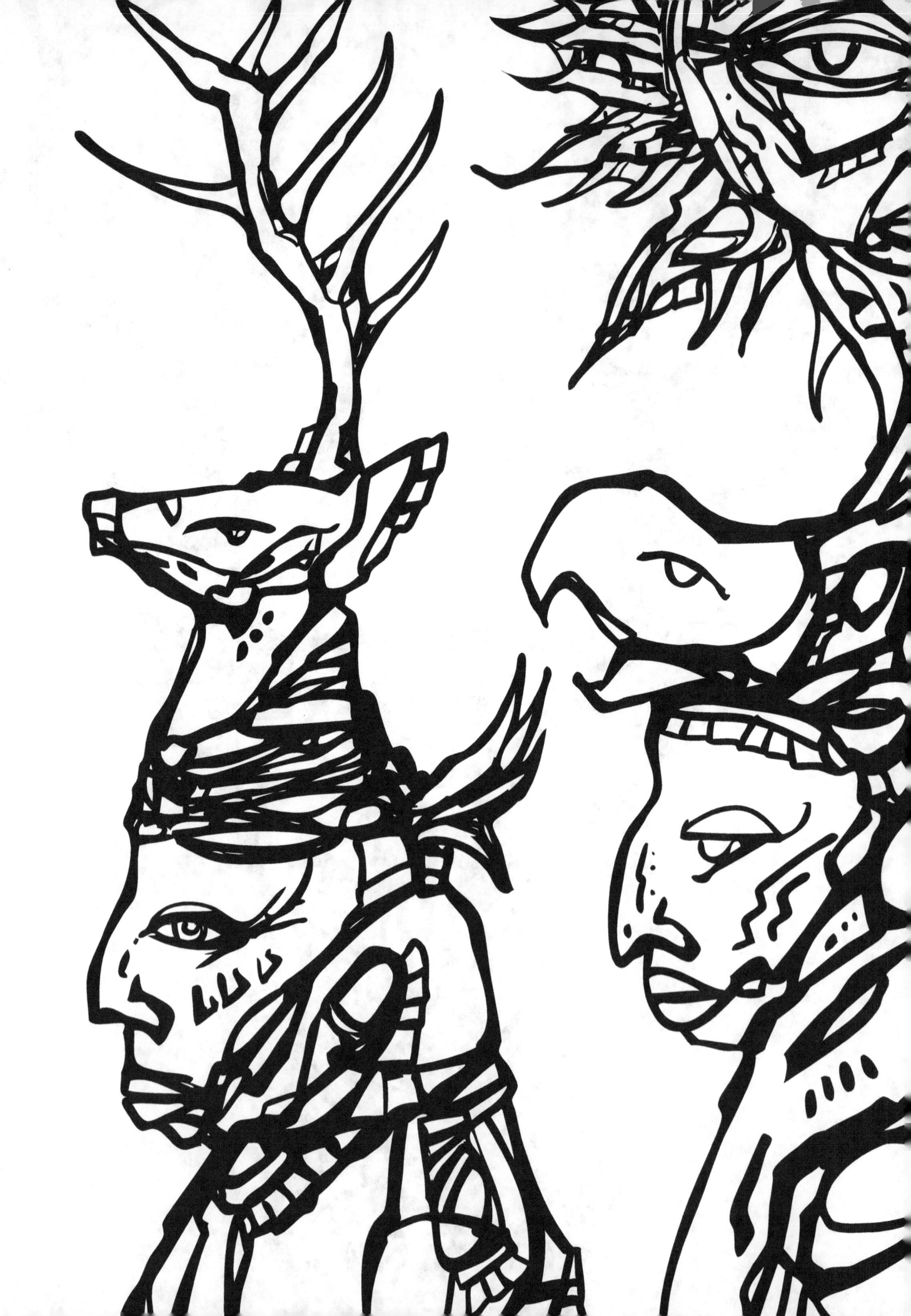

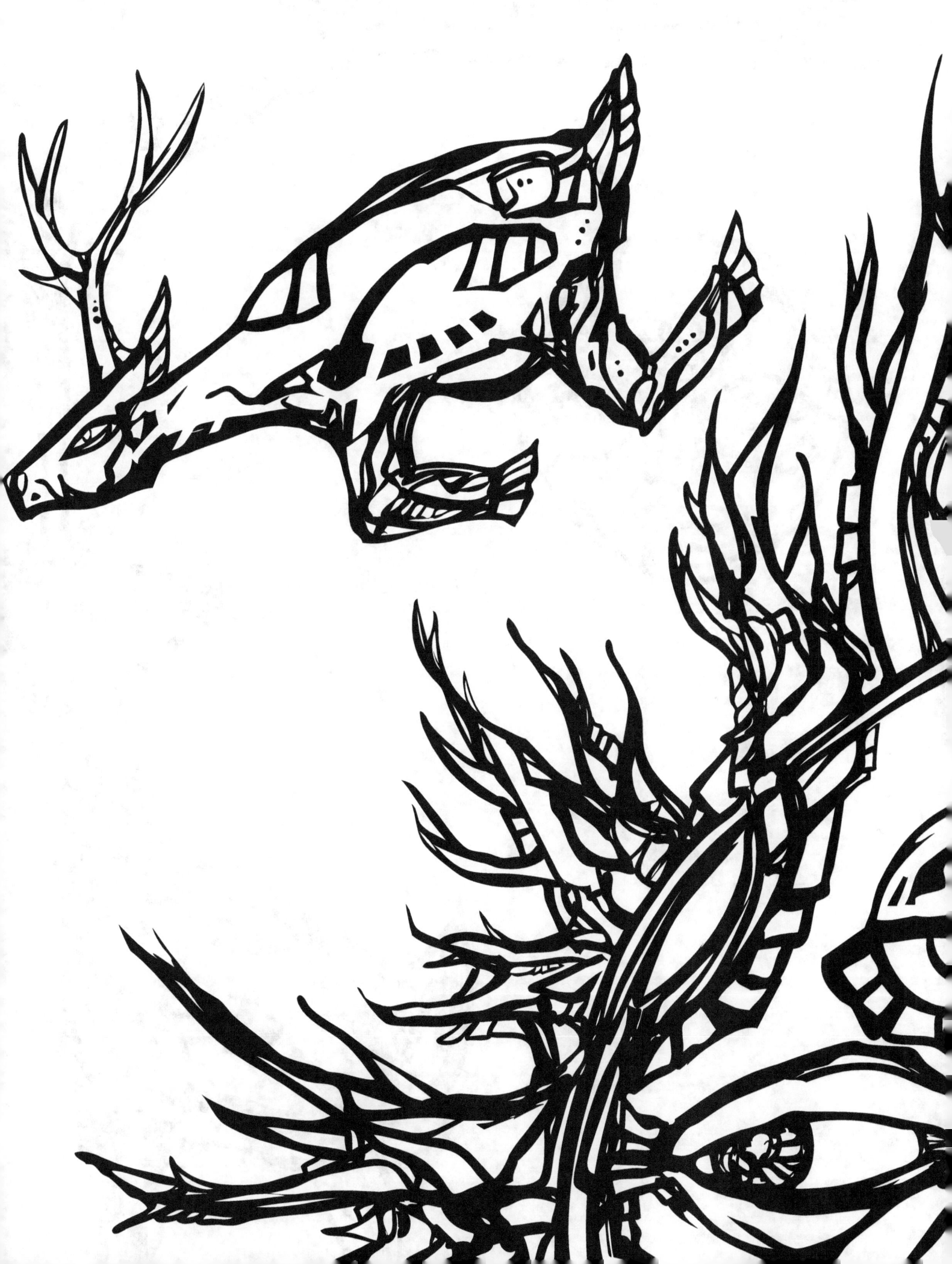

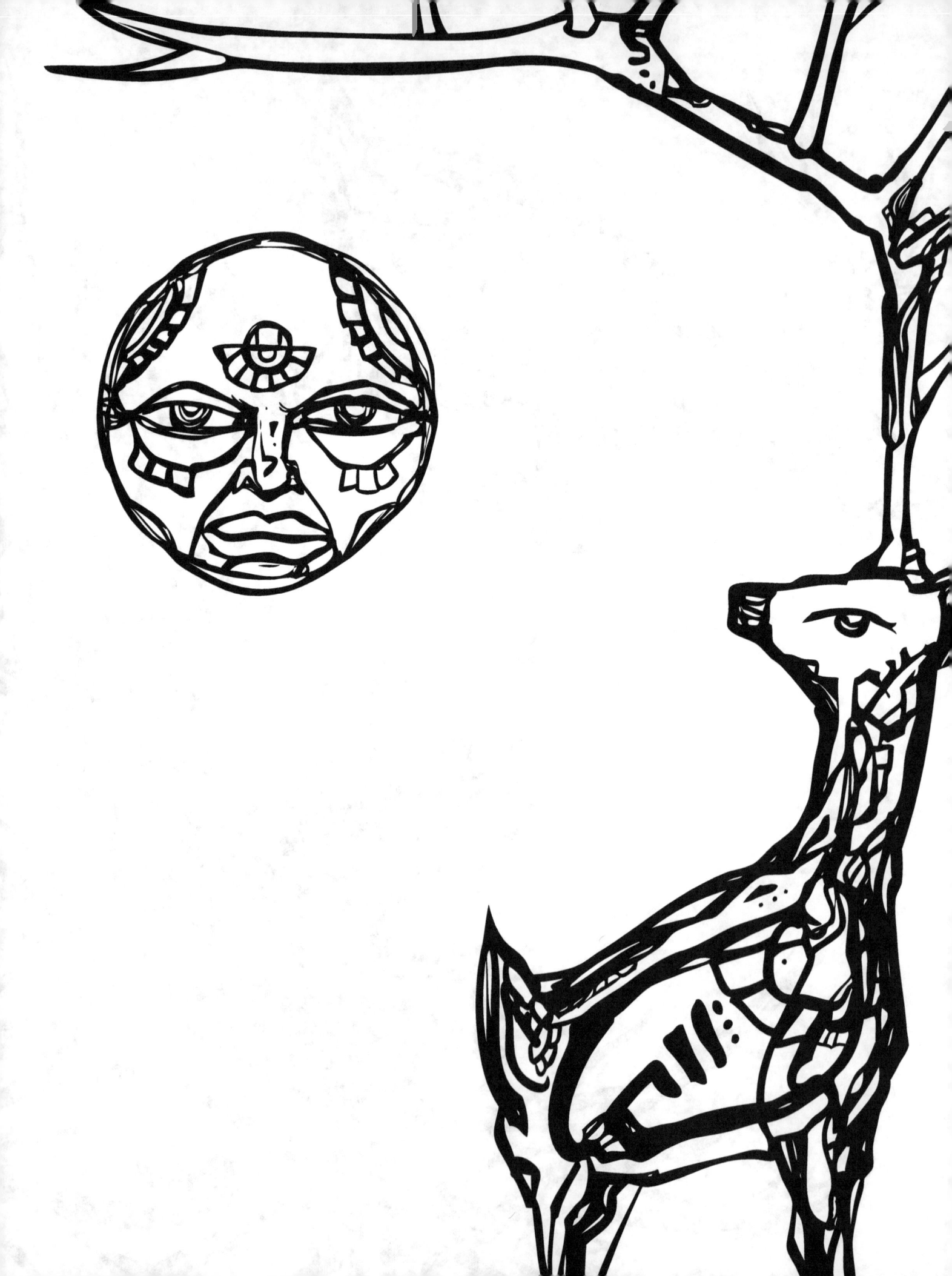

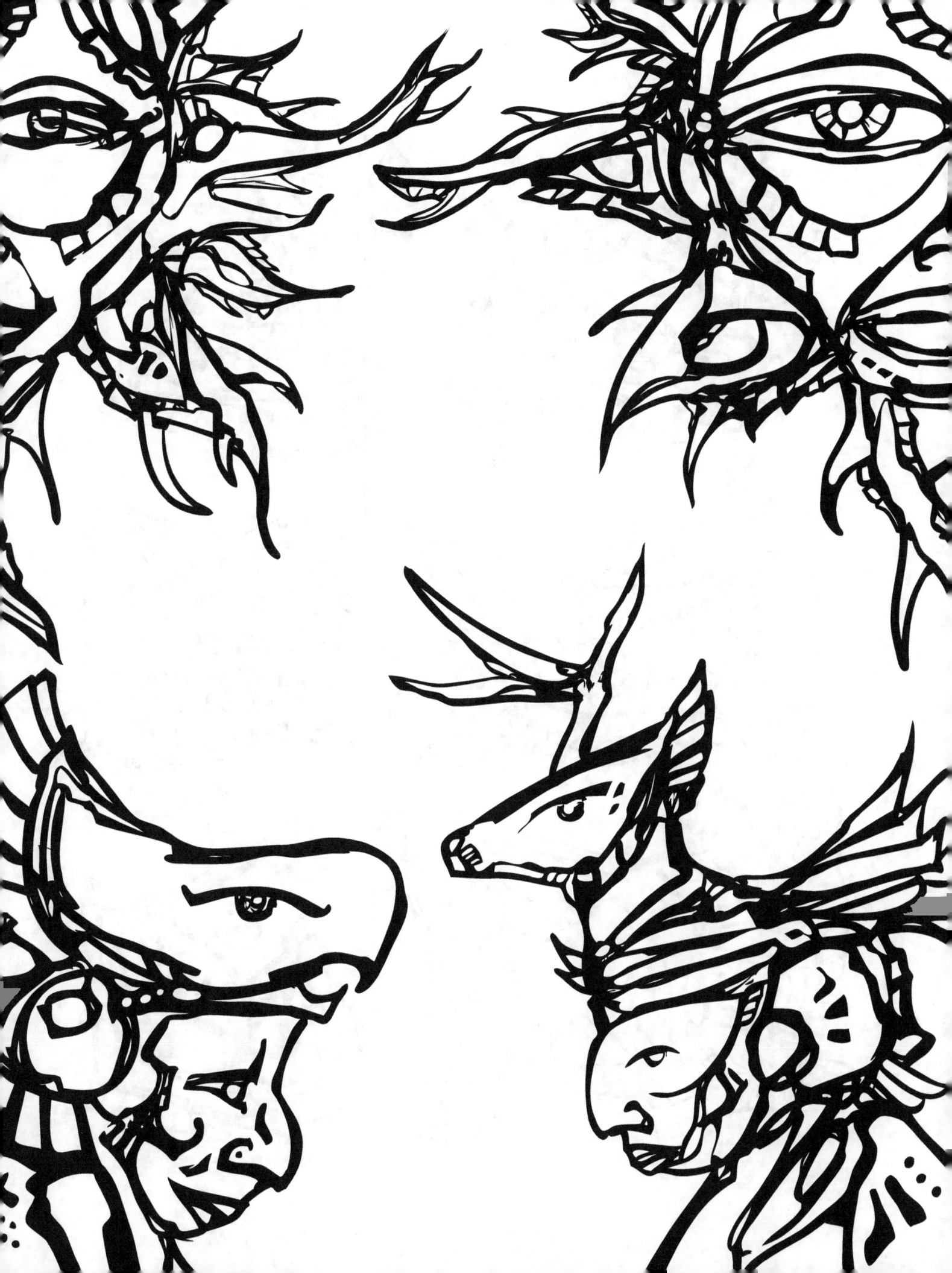

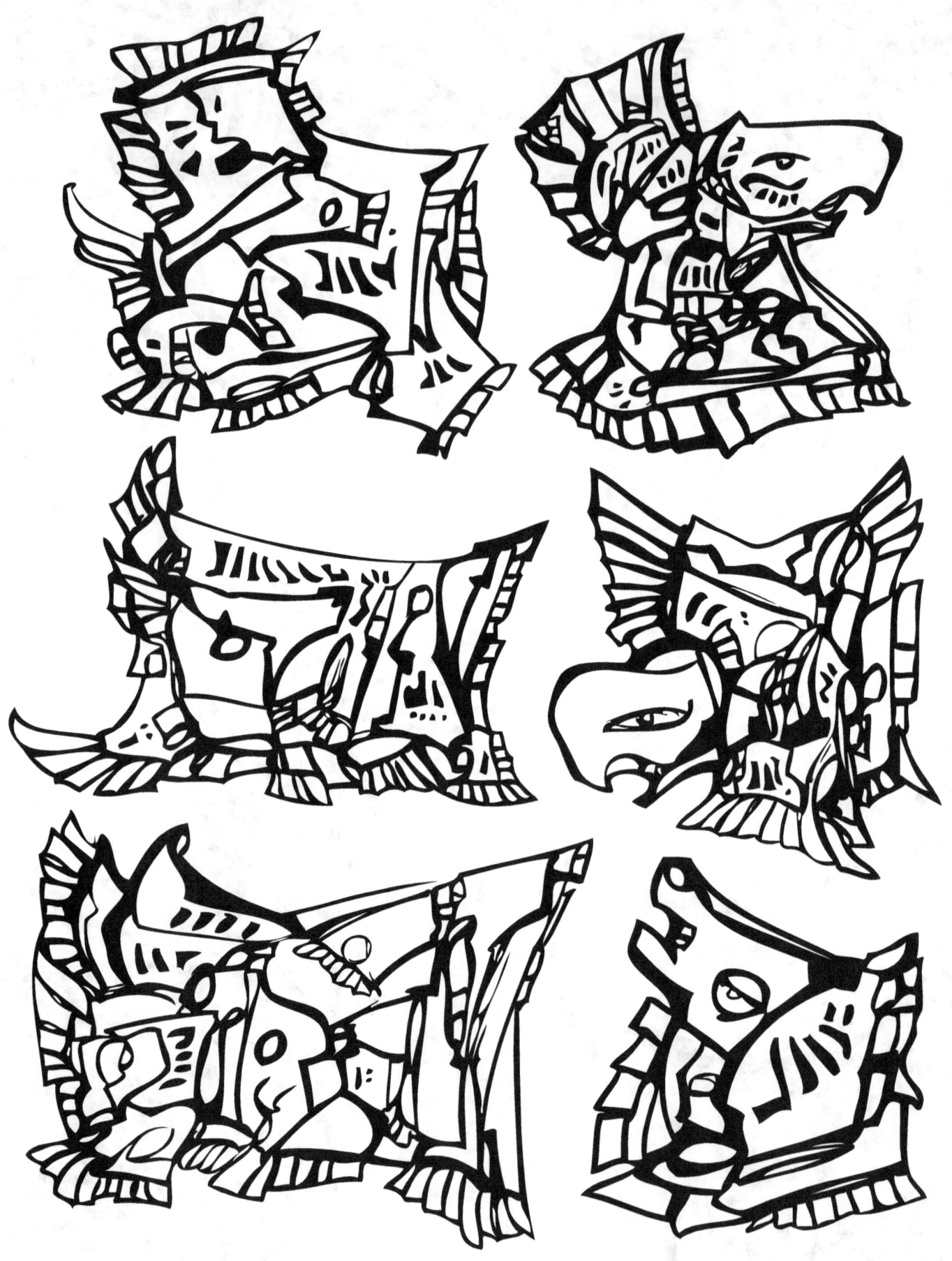

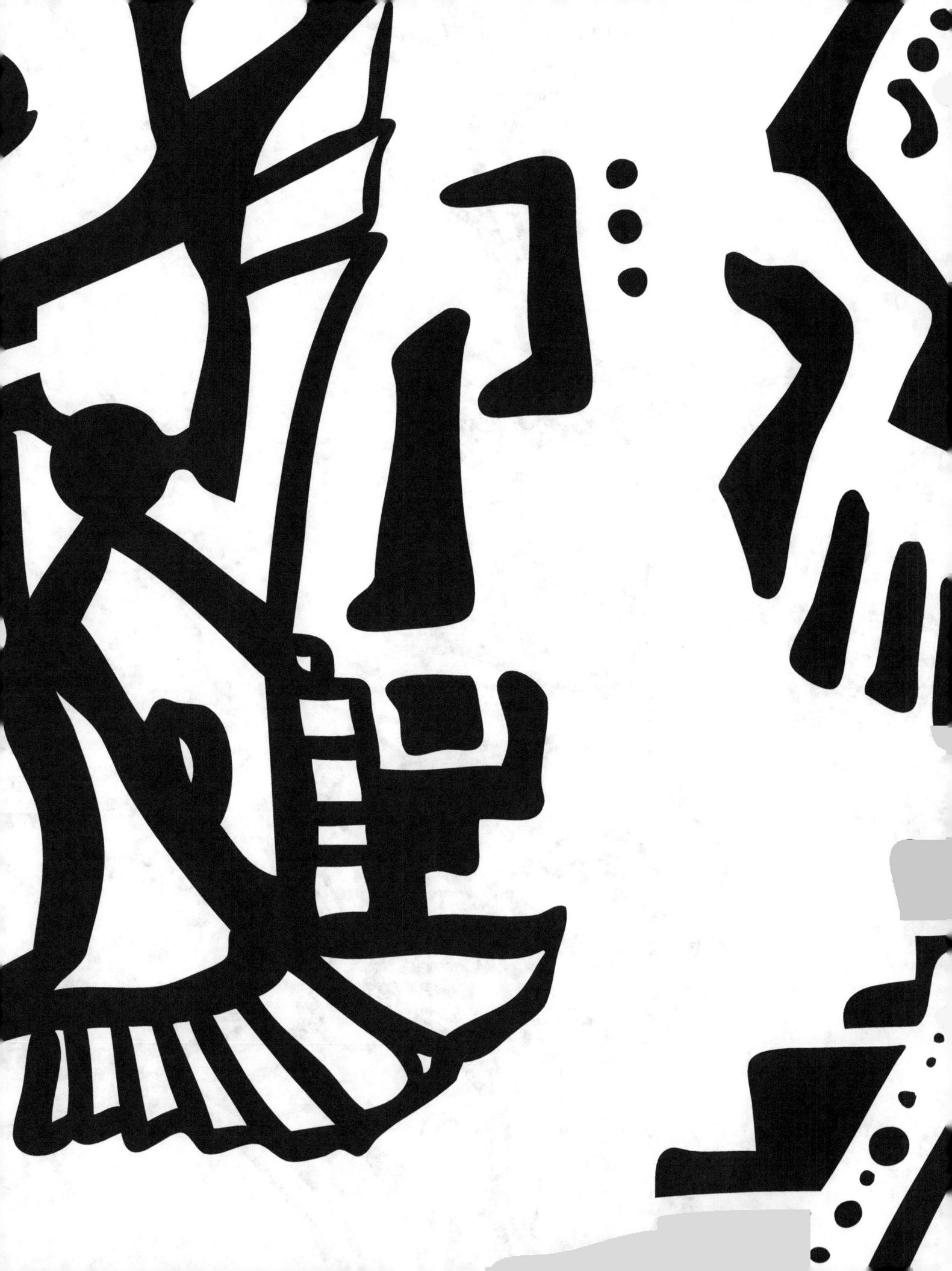

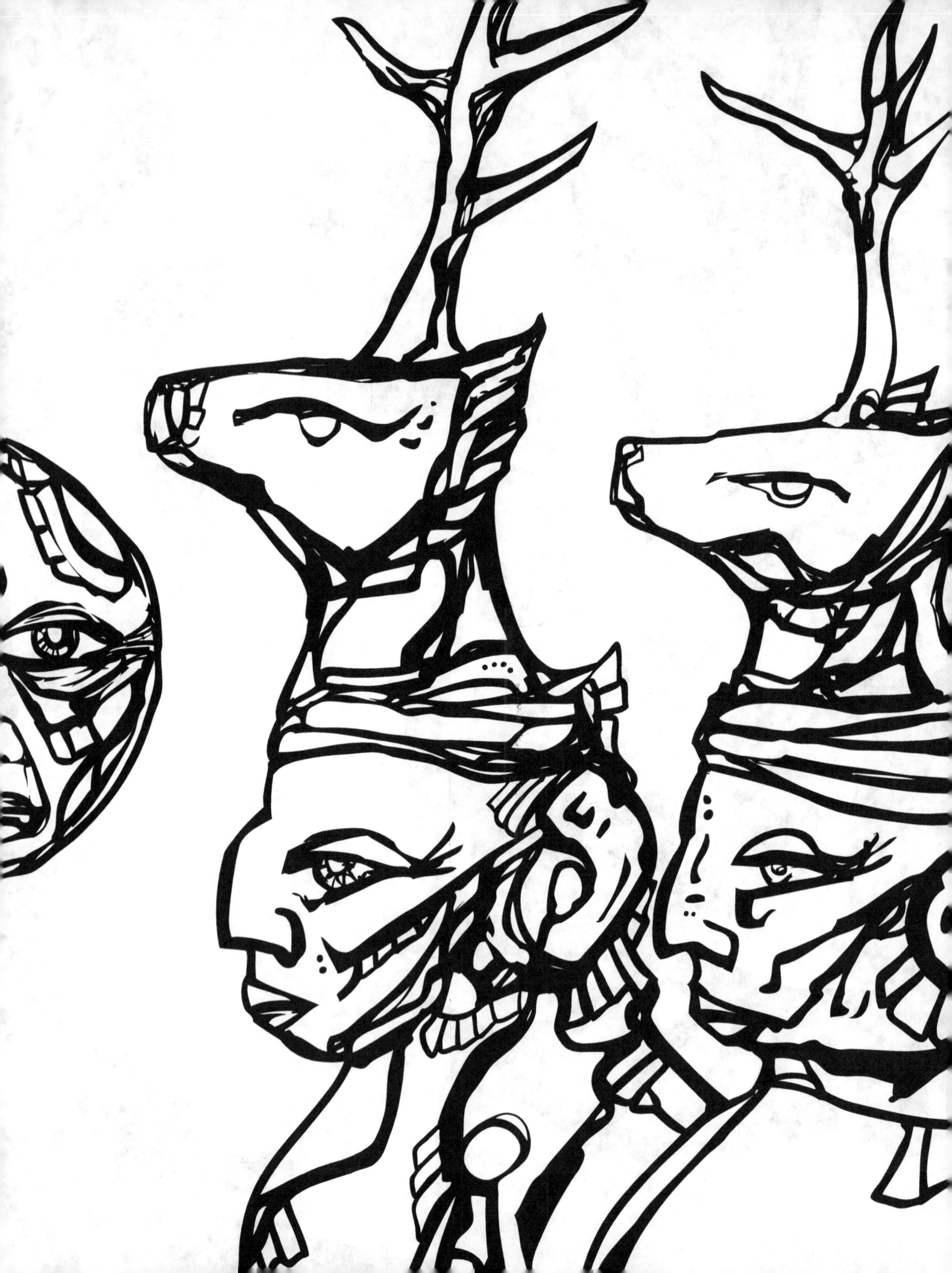

The Purpose of this book is simply to ignite memory. To help recollect and re-member genetic realties. This is not simply a coloring book. It is a space of creating. Let the colors you bring to this book bring you vision and insight. Spark your own drawings. These drawing were part of a series of drawings that were 1000 that started with using Sharpie markers and ended with a wacom tablet. The reason why i chose 1000 and Sharpies is because in my neighborhood Sharpies are used at times to create art on walls, buses, desks, bathrooms, but sometimes they are used to deface property. So in essence it was a way to hand back to my neighborhood another means of using this marker. The reason why i choose 1000 is part of a prayer for abundance. Part of a prayer where there is fear of scarcity. We are not poor. We are rich. We have infinite creativity. We have infinite vision. We are not limited in our capacities but somewhere along the lines we forgot. We have forgotten how to be children. We have forgotten all the wisdom and knowledge that is brought unto us when we remain in that beauty and childlike innocence and playfulness. We have learned to develop alot of bad habits that don't service. So i hope that this Codex serves at a space of re-membering. re-structuring and reconstructing. I hope that this space is a place for WEAPONS OF MASS CREATION, because this world needs it. Your home needs it. Your walk and your life need it. You need it. I need it. And we have it. In our everyday opportunities to give back random acts of kindness. random acts of compassion and love. So hopefully this codex inspired your own endevours into asemic writing. codex writing. grafitti writing. street art. cave art. all art writing. Because whatever your culture is. You have ancestors. Who believed in some very basic fundamental truths. Whether you have druid, mayan, tolteca, african, european ancestry, there are some core connections embedded in their wisdom. Follow their trail. Follow it with your heart. With the intelligence of your highest self. And connect with them. The earth and all the beings that are a precious part of you. And you apart of them.

Tlazokamati

Israel